A Critical History Of Greek Philosophy

By
W. T. Stace

A CRITICAL HISTORY OF GREEK PHILOSOPHY

CHAPTER I

THE IDEA OF PHILOSOPHY IN GENERAL.

THE ORIGINS AND DEVELOPMENT OF GREEK PHILOSOPHY

It is natural that, at the commencement of any study, one should be expected to say what the subject-matter of that study is. Botany is the knowledge of plants, astronomy of the heavenly bodies, geology of the rocks of the earth's crust. What, then, is the special sphere of philosophy? What is philosophy about? Now it is not as easy to give a concise definition of philosophy, as it is of the other sciences. In the first place, the content of philosophy has differed considerably in different periods of history. In general the tendency has been to narrow down the scope of the subject as knowledge advanced, to exclude from philosophy what was formerly included in it. Thus in the time of Plato, physics and astronomy were included as parts of philosophy, whereas now they constitute separate sciences. This, however, is not an insurmountable difficulty. What chiefly militates against the effort to frame a definition is that the precise content of philosophy is differently viewed by different schools of thought. Thus a definition of philosophy which a follower of Herbert Spencer might frame would be unacceptable to an Hegelian, and the Hegelian definition would be rejected by the Spencerian. If we were to include in our definition some such phrase as "the knowledge of the Absolute," while this might suit some philosophers, others would deny that there is any Absolute at all. Another school would say that there may be an Absolute, but that it is unknowable, so that philosophy cannot be the knowledge of it. Yet another school would tell us that, whether there is or is not an Absolute, whether it is or is not knowable, the knowledge of it is in any case useless, and ought not to be sought. Hence no definition of philosophy can be appreciated without some knowledge of the special tenets of the various schools. In a word, the proper place to give a definition is not at the beginning of the study of philosophy, but at the end of it. Then, with all views before us, we might be able to decide the question.

I shall make no attempt, therefore, to place before you a precise definition. But perhaps the same purpose will be served, if I pick out some of the leading traits of philosophy, which serve to distinguish it from other branches of knowledge, and illustrate them by enumerating--but without any attempt at completeness--some of the chief problems which philosophers have usually attempted to solve. And firstly, philosophy is distinguished from other branches of knowledge by the fact that, whereas these each take some particular portion of the universe for their study, philosophy does not specialize in this way, but deals with the universe as a whole. The universe is one, and ideal knowledge of it would be one; but the principles of specialization and division of labour apply here as elsewhere, and so astronomy takes for its subject that portion of the universe which we call the heavenly bodies, botany specializes in plant life, psychology in the facts of the mind, and so on. But philosophy does not deal with this or that particular sphere of being, but with being as such. It seeks to see the universe as a single co-ordinated system of things. It might be described as the science of things in general. The world in its most universal aspects is its subject. All sciences tend to generalize, to reduce multitudes of particular facts to single general laws. Philosophy carries this process to its highest limit. It generalizes to the utmost. It seeks to view the entire universe in the light of the fewest possible general principles, in the light, if possible, of a single ultimate principle.

It is a consequence of this that the special sciences take their subject matter, and much of their contents, for granted, whereas philosophy seeks to trace everything back to its ultimate grounds. It may be thought that this description of the sciences is incorrect. Is not the essential maxim of modern science to assume nothing, to take nothing for granted, to assert nothing without demonstration, to prove all? This is no doubt true within certain limits, but beyond those limits it does not hold good. All the sciences take quite for granted certain principles and facts which are, for them, ultimate. To investigate these is the portion of the philosopher, and philosophy thus takes up the thread of knowledge where the sciences drop it. It begins where they end. It investigates what they take as a matter of course.

Let us consider some examples of this. The science of geometry deals with the laws of space. But it takes space just as it finds it in common experience. It takes space for granted. No geometrician asks what space is. This, then, will be a problem for philosophy. Moreover, geometry is founded upon certain fundamental propositions which, it asserts, being self-evident, require no investigation. These are called "axioms." That two straight lines cannot enclose a space, and that equals being added to equals the results are equal, are common examples. Into the ground of these axioms the geometrician does not enquire. That is the business of philosophy. Not that philosophers affect to doubt the truth of these axioms. But surely it is a very strange thing, and a fact quite worthy of study, that there are some statements of which we feel that we must give the most laborious proofs, and others in the case of which we feel no such necessity. How is it that some propositions can be self-evident and others must be proved? What is the ground of this distinction? And when one comes to think of it, it is a very extraordinary property of mind that it should be able to make the most universal and unconditional statements about things, without a jot of evidence or proof. When we say that two straight lines cannot enclose a space, we do not mean merely that this has been found true in regard to all the particular pairs of straight lines with which we have tried the experiment. We mean that it never can be and never has been otherwise. We mean that a million million years ago two straight lines did not enclose a space, and that it will be the same a million million years hence, and that it is just as true on those stars, if there are any, which are invisible even to the greatest telescopes. But we have no experience of what will happen a million million years hence, or of what can take place among those remote stars. And yet we assert, with absolute confidence, that our axiom is and must be equally true everywhere and at all times. Moreover, we do not found this on probabilities gathered from experience. Nobody would make experiments or use telescopes to prove such axioms. How is it that they are thus self-evident, that the mind can make these definite and far-reaching assertions without any evidence at all? Geometricians do not consider these questions. They take the facts for granted. To solve these problems is for philosophy.

Again, the physical sciences take the existence of matter for granted. But philosophy asks what matter is. At first sight it might appear that this question is one for the physicist and not the philosopher. For the problem of "the constitution of matter" is a well-known physical problem. But a little consideration will show that this is quite a different question from the one the philosopher propounds. For even if it be shown that all matter is ether, or electricity, or vortex-atoms, or other such, this does not help us in our special problem. For these theories, even if proved, only teach us that the different kinds of matter are forms of some one physical existence. But what we want to know is what physical existence itself is. To prove that one kind of matter is really another kind of matter does not tell us what is the essential nature of matter. That, therefore, is a problem, not of science, but of philosophy.

In the same way, all the sciences take the existence of the universe for granted. But philosophy seeks to know why it is that there is a universe at all. Is it true, for example, that there is some single ultimate reality which produces all things? And if so, what sort of a reality is it? Is it matter, or mind, or something different from both? Is it good or evil? And if it is good, how is it that there is evil in the world?

Moreover every science, except the purely mathematical sciences, assumes the truth of the law of causation. Every student of logic knows that this is the ultimate canon of the sciences, the foundation of them all. If we did not believe in the truth of the law of causation, namely, that everything which has a beginning has a cause, and that in the same circumstances the same things invariably happen, all the sciences would at once crumble to dust. In every scientific investigation, this truth is assumed. If we ask the zoologist how he knows that all camels are herbivorous, he will no doubt point in the first instance to experience. The habits of many thousands of camels have been observed. But this only proves that those particular camels are herbivorous. How about the millions that have never been observed at all? He can only appeal to the law of causation. The camel's structure is such that it cannot digest meat. It is a case of cause and effect. How do we know that water always freezes at 0° centigrade (neglecting questions of pressure, etc.)? How do we know that this is true at those regions of the earth where no one has ever been to see? Only because we believe that in the same circumstances the same thing always happens, that like causes always produce like effects. But how do we know the truth of this law of causation itself? Science does not consider the question. It traces its assertions back to this law, but goes no further. Its fundamental canon it takes for granted. The grounds of causation, why it is true, and how we know it is true, are, therefore, philosophical questions.

One may be tempted to enquire whether many of these questions, especially those connected with the ultimate reality, do not transcend human faculties altogether, and whether we had not better confine our enquiries to matters that are not "too high for us." One may question whether it is possible for finite minds to comprehend the infinite. Now it is very right that such questions should be asked, and it is essential that a correct answer should be found. But, for the present, there is nothing to say about the matter, except that these questions themselves constitute one of the most important problems of philosophy, though it is one which, as a matter of fact, has scarcely been considered in full until modern times. The Greeks did not raise the question. And as this is itself one of the problems of philosophy, it will be well to start with an open mind. The question cannot be decided offhand, but must be thoroughly investigated. That the finite mind of man cannot understand the infinite is one of those popular dogmatic assertions, which are bruited about from mouth to mouth, as if they were self-evident, and so come to tyrannize over men's minds. But for the most part those who make this statement have never thoroughly sifted the grounds of it, but simply take it as something universally admitted, and trouble no further about it. But at the very least we should first know exactly what we mean by such terms as "mind," "finite," and "infinite." And we shall not find that our difficulties end even there.

Philosophy, then, deals with the universe as a whole; and it seeks to take nothing for granted. A third characteristic may be noted as especially important, though here no doubt we are trenching upon matters upon which there is no such universal agreement. Philosophy is essentially an attempt to rise from sensuous to pure, that is, non-senuous, thought. This requires some explanation.

We are conscious, so to speak, of two different worlds, the external physical world and the internal mental world. If we look outwards we are aware of the former, if we turn our gaze inwards upon our own minds we become aware of the latter. It may appear incorrect to say that the external world is purely physical, for it includes other minds. I am aware of your mind, and this is, to me, part of the world which is external to me. But I am not now speaking of what we know by inference, but only of what we directly perceive. I cannot directly perceive your mind, but only your physical body. In the last resort it will be found that I am aware of the existence of your mind only by inference from perceived physical facts, such as the movements of your body and the sounds that issue from your lips. The only mind which I can immediately perceive is my own. There is then a physical world external to us, and an internal mental world.

Which of these will naturally be regarded as the most real? Men will regard as the most real that which is the most familiar, that which they came first into contact with, and have most experience of. And this is unquestionably the external material world. When a child is born, it turns its eyes to the light, which is an external physical thing. Gradually it gets to know different objects in the room. It comes to know its mother, but its mother is, in the first instance, a physical object, a body. It is only long afterwards that its mother becomes for the child a mind or a soul. In general, all our earliest experiences are of the material world. We come to know of the mental world only by introspection, and the habit of introspection comes in youth or manhood only, and to many people it hardly comes at all. In all those early impressionable years, therefore, when our most durable ideas of the universe are formed, we are concerned almost exclusively with the material world. The mental world with which we are much less familiar consequently tends to appear to all of us something comparatively unreal, a world of shadows. The bent of our minds becomes materialistic.

What I have said of the individual is equally true of the race. Primitive man does not brood over the facts of his own mind. Necessity compels him to devote most of his life to the acquisition of food, and to warding off the dangers which continually threaten him from other physical objects. And even among ourselves, the majority of men have to spend most of their time upon considering various aspects of things external to them. By the individual training of each man, and by long hereditary habit, then, it comes about that men tend to regard the physical world as more real than the mental.

Abundant evidences of this are to be found in the structure of human language. We seek to explain what is strange by means of what is well-known. We try to express the unfamiliar in terms of the familiar. We shall find that language always seeks to express the mental by the analogy of the physical. We speak of a man as a "clear" thinker. "Clear" is an attribute of physical objects. Water is clear if it has no extraneous matter in it. We say that a man's ideas are "luminous," thus taking a metaphor from physical light. We talk of having an idea "at the back of the mind." "At the back of"? Has the mind got a front and a back? We are thinking of it as if it were a physical thing in space. We speak of mental habits of "attention." "Attention" means stretching or turning the mind in a special direction. We "reflect." "Reflection" means bending our thoughts back upon themselves. But, literally speaking, only physical objects can be stretched, turned, and bent. Whenever we wish to express something mental we do it by a physical analogy. We talk of it in terms of physical things. This shows how deep-rooted our materialism is. If the mental world were more familiar and real to us than the material, language would have been constructed on the opposite principle. The earliest words of language would have expressed mental facts, and we should afterwards have tried to express physical things by means of mental analogies.

In the East one commonly hears Oriental idealism contrasted with Western materialism. Such phrases may possess a certain relative truth. But if they mean that there is in the East, or anywhere else in the world, a race of men who are naturally idealists, they are nonsense. Materialism is ingrained in all men. We, Easterns or Westerns, are born materialists. Hence when we try to think of objects which are commonly regarded as non-material, such as God or the soul, it requires continual effort, a tremendous struggle, to avoid picturing them as material things. It goes utterly against the grain. Perhaps hundreds of thousands of years of hereditary materialism are against us. The popular idea of ghosts will illustrate this. Those who believe in ghosts, I suppose, regard them as some sort of disembodied souls. The pictures of ghosts in magazines show them as if composed of matter, but matter of some thin kind, such as vapour. Certain Indian systems of thought, which are by way of regarding themselves as idealistic, nevertheless teach that thought or mind is an extremely subtle kind of matter, far subtler than any ever dealt with by the physicist and chemist. This is very interesting, because it shows that the authors of such ideas feel vaguely that it is wrong to think of thought as if it were matter, but being unable to think of it in any other way, owing to man's ingrained materialism, they seek to palliate their sin by making it thin matter. Of course this is just as absurd as the excuse made by the mother of an illegitimate child, that it was a very small one. This thin matter is just as material as lead or brass. And such systems are purely materialistic. But they illustrate the extraordinary difficulty that the ordinary mind experiences in attempting to rise from sensuous to non-sensuous thinking. They illustrate the ingrained materialism of man.

This natural human materialism is also the cause of mysticism and symbolism. A symbolic thought necessarily contains two terms, the symbol and the reality which it symbolizes. The symbol is always a sensuous or material object, or the mental image of such an object, and the reality is always something non-sensuous. Because the human mind finds it such an incredible struggle to think non-sensuously, it seeks to help itself by symbols. It takes a material thing and makes it stand for the non-material thing which it is too weak to grasp. Thus we talk of God as the "light of lights." No doubt this is a very natural expression of the religious consciousness, and it has its meaning. But it is not the naked truth. Light is a physical existence, and God is no more light than he is heat or electricity. People talk of symbolism as if it were a very high and exalted thing. They say, "What a wonderful piece of symbolism!" But, in truth symbolism is the mark of an infirm mind. It is the measure of our weakness and not of our strength. Its root is in materialism, and it is produced and propagated by those who are unable to rise above a materialistic level.

Now philosophy is essentially the attempt to get beyond this sort of symbolic and mystical thinking, to get at the naked truth, to grasp what lies behind the symbol as it is in itself. These inferior modes of thought are a help to those who are themselves below their level, but are a hindrance to those who seek to reach the highest level of truth.

It is often said that philosophy is a very difficult and abstruse subject. Its difficulty lies almost wholly in the struggle to think non-sensuously. Whenever we come to anything in philosophy that seems beyond us, we shall generally find that the root of the trouble is that we are trying to think non-sensuous objects in a sensuous way, that is, we are trying to form mental pictures and images of them, for all mental pictures are composed of sensuous materials, and hence no such picture is adequate for a pure thought. It is impossible to exaggerate this difficulty. Even the greatest philosophers have succumbed to it. We shall constantly have to point out that when a great thinker, such as Parmenides or Plato, fails, and begins to flounder in difficulties, the reason usually is that, though for a time he has attained to pure thought, he has sunk back exhausted into sensuous thinking, and has attempted to form mental pictures of what is beyond the power of any such picture to represent, and so has fallen into contradictions. We must keep this constantly in mind in the study of philosophy.

In modern times philosophy is variously divided, as into metaphysics, which is the theory of reality, ethics, the theory of the good, and aesthetics, the theory of the beautiful. Modern divisions do not, however, altogether fit in with Greek philosophy, and it is better to let the natural divisions develop themselves as we go on, than to attempt to force our material into these moulds.

If, now, we look round the world and ask; in what countries and what ages the kind of thought we have described has attained a high degree of development, we shall find such a development only in ancient Greece and in modern Europe. There were great civilizations in Egypt, China, Assyria, and so on. They produced art and religion, but no philosophy to speak of. Even ancient Rome added nothing to the world's philosophical knowledge. Its so-called philosophers, Marcus Aurelius, Seneca, Epictetus, Lucretius, produced no essentially new principle. They were merely disciples of Greek Schools, whose writings may be full of interest and of noble feeling, but whose essential thoughts contained nothing not already developed by the Greeks.

The case of India is more doubtful. Opinions may differ as to whether India ever had any philosophy. The Upanishads contain religio-philosophical thinking of a kind. And later we have the six so-called schools of philosophy. The reasons why this Indian thought is not usually included in histories of philosophy are as follows. Firstly, philosophy in India has never separated itself from religious and practical needs. The ideal of knowledge for its own sake is rarely to be found. Knowledge is desired merely as a means towards salvation. Philosophy and science, said Aristotle, have their roots in wonder,--the desire to know and understand for the sole sake of knowing and understanding. But the roots of Indian thought lie in the anxiety of the individual to escape from the ills and calamities of existence. This is not the scientific, but the practical spirit. It gives birth to religions, but not to philosophies. Of course it is a mistake to imagine that philosophy and religion are totally separate and have no community. They are in fact fundamentally akin. But they are also distinct. Perhaps the truest view is that they are identical in substance, but different in form. The substance of both is the absolute reality and the relation of all things, including men, to that reality. But whereas philosophy presents this subject-matter scientifically, in the form of pure thought, religion gives it in the form of sensuous pictures, myths, images, and symbols.

And this gives us the second reason why Indian thought is more properly classed as religious than philosophical. It seldom or never rises from sensuous to pure thought. It is poetical rather than scientific. It is content with symbols and metaphors in place of rational explanations, and all this is a mark of the religious, rather than the philosophical, presentation of the truth. For example, the main thought of the Upanishads is that the entire universe is derived from a single, changeless, eternal, infinite, being, called Brahman or Paramatman. When we come to the crucial question how the universe arises out of this being, we find such passages as this:--"As the colours in the flame or the red-hot iron proceed therefrom a thousand-fold, so do all beings proceed from the Unchangeable, and return again to it." Or again, "As the web issues from the spider, as little sparks proceed from fire, so from the one soul proceed all living animals, all worlds, all the gods and all beings." There are thousands of such passages in the Upanishads. But obviously these neither explain nor attempt to explain anything. They are nothing but hollow metaphors. They are poetic rather than scientific. They may satisfy the imagination and the religious feelings, but not the rational understanding. Or when again Krishna, in the Bhagavat-Gita, describes himself as the moon among the lunar mansions, the sun among the stars, Meru among the high-peaked mountains, it is clear that we are merely piling sensuous image upon sensuous image without any further understanding of what the nature of the absolute being in its own self is. The moon, the sun, Meru, are physical sense-objects. And this is totally sensuous thinking, whereas the aim of philosophy is to rise to pure thought. In such passages we are still on the level of symbolism, and philosophy only begins when symbolism has been surpassed. No doubt it is possible to take the line that man's thought is not capable of grasping the infinite as it is in itself, and can only fall back upon symbols. But that is another question, and at any rate, whether it is or is not possible to rise from sensuous to pure thought, philosophy is essentially the attempt to do so.

Lastly, Indian thought is usually excluded from the history of philosophy because, whatever its character, it lies outside the main stream of human development. It has been cut off by geographical and other barriers. Consequently, whatever its value in itself, it has exerted little influence upon philosophy in general.

The claim is sometimes put forward by Orientals themselves that Greek philosophy came from India, and if this were true, it would greatly affect the statement made in the last paragraph. But it is not true. It used to be believed that Greek philosophy came from "the East," but this meant Egypt. And even this theory is now abandoned. Greek culture, especially mathematics and astronomy, owed much to Egypt. But Greece did not owe its philosophy to that source. The view that it did was propagated by Alexandrian priests and others, whose sole motive was, that to represent the triumphs of Greek philosophy as borrowed from Egypt, flattered their national vanity. It was a great thing, wherever they found anything good, to say, "this must have come from us." A precisely similar motive lies behind the Oriental claim that Greek philosophy came from India. There is not a scrap of evidence for it, and it rests entirely upon the supposed resemblance between the two. But this resemblance is in fact mythical. The whole character of Greek philosophy is European and unoriental to the back-bone. The doctrine of re-incarnation is usually appealed to. This characteristically Indian doctrine was held by the Pythagoreans, from whom it passed to Empedocles and Plato. The Pythagoreans got it from the Orphic sect, to whom quite possibly it came indirectly from India, although even this is by no means certain, and is in fact highly doubtful. But even if this be true, it proves nothing. Re-incarnation is of little importance in Greek philosophy. Even in Plato, who makes much of it, it is quite unessential to the fundamental ideas of his philosophy, and is only artificially connected with them. And the influence of this doctrine upon Plato's philosophy was thoroughly bad. It was largely responsible for leading him into the main error of his philosophy, which it required an Aristotle to correct. All this will be evident when we come to consider the systems of Plato and Aristotle.

The origin of Greek philosophy is not to be found in India, or Egypt, or in any country outside Greece. The Greeks themselves were solely responsible for it. It is not as if history traces back their thought only to a point at which it was already highly developed, and cannot explain its beginnings. We know its history from the time, so to speak, when it was in the cradle. In the next two chapters we shall see that the first Greek attempts at philosophising were so much the beginnings of a beginner, were so very crude and unformed, that it is mere perversity to suppose that they could not make these simple efforts for themselves. From those crude beginnings we can trace the whole development in detail up to its culmination in Aristotle, and beyond. So there is no need to assume foreign influence at any point.

Greek philosophy begins in the sixth century before Christ. It begins when men for the first time attempted to give a scientific reply to the question, "what is the explanation of the world?" Before this era we have, of course, the mythologies, cosmogonies, and theologies of the poets. But they contain no attempt at a naturalistic explanation of things. They belong to the spheres of poetry and religion, not to philosophy.

It must not be supposed, when we speak of the philosophy of Greece, that we refer only to the mainland of what is now called Greece. Very early in history, Greeks of the mainland migrated to the islands of the Aegean, to Sicily, to the South of Italy, to the coast of Asia Minor, and elsewhere, and founded flourishing colonies. The Greece of philosophy includes all these places. It is to be thought of rather racially than territorially. It is the philosophy of the men of Greek race, wherever they happened to be situated. And in fact the first period of Greek philosophy deals exclusively with the thoughts of these colonial Greeks. It was not till just before the time of Socrates that philosophy was transplanted to the mainland.

Greek philosophy falls naturally into three periods. The first may be roughly described as pre-Socratic philosophy, though it does not include the Sophists who were both the contemporaries and the predecessors of Socrates. This period is the rise of Greek philosophy. Secondly, the period from the Sophists to Aristotle, which includes Socrates and Plato, is the maturity of Greek philosophy, the actual zenith and culmination of which is undoubtedly the system of Aristotle. Lastly, the period of post-Aristotelian philosophy constitutes the decline and fall of the national thought. These are not merely arbitrary divisions. Each period has its own special characters, which will be described in the sequel.

A few words must be said of the sources of our knowledge of pre-Socratic philosophy. If we want to know what Plato and Aristotle thought about any matter, we have only to consult their works. But the works of the earlier philosophers have not come down to us, except in fragments, and several of them never committed their opinions to writing. Our knowledge of their doctrines is the result of the laborious sifting by scholars of such materials as are available. Luckily the material has been plentiful. It may be divided into three classes. First come the fragments of the original writings of the philosophers themselves. These are in many cases long and important, in other cases scanty. Secondly, there are the references in Plato and Aristotle. Of these by far the most important are to be found in the first book of Aristotle's "Metaphysics," which is a history of philosophy up to his own time, and is the first attempt on record to write a history of philosophy. Thirdly, there is an enormous mass of references, some valuable, some worthless, contained in the works of later, but still ancient, writers.

CHAPTER II
THE IONICS.

The earliest Greek philosophers belong to what in after times came to be called the Ionic school. The name was derived from the fact that the three chief representatives of this school, Thales, Anaximander, and Anaximenes, were all men of Ionia, that is to say, the coast of Asia Minor.

Thales

As the founder of the earliest school in history, Thales of Miletus is generally accounted the founder and father of all philosophy. He was born about 624 B.C. and died about 550 B.C. These dates are approximate, and it should be understood that the same thing is true of nearly all the dates of the early philosophers. Different scholars vary, sometimes as much as ten years, in the dates they give. We shall not enter into these questions at all, because they are of no importance. And throughout these lectures it should be understood that the dates given are approximate.

Thales, at any rate, was a contemporary of Solon and Croesus. He was famous in antiquity for his mathematical and astronomical learning, and also for his practical sagacity and wisdom. He is included in all the accounts of the Seven Sages. The story of the Seven Sages is unhistorical, but the fact that the lists of their names differ considerably as given by different writers, whereas the name of Thales appears in all, shows with what veneration he was anciently regarded. An eclipse of the sun occurred in 585 B.C., and Thales is alleged to have predicted it, which was a feat for the astronomy of those times. And he must have been a great engineer, for he caused a diversion of the river Halys, when Croesus and his army were unable to cross it. Nothing else is known of his life, though there were many apocryphal stories.

No writings by Thales were extant even in the time of Aristotle, and it is believed that he wrote nothing. His philosophy, if we can call it by that name, consisted, so far as we know, of two propositions. Firstly, that the principle of all things is water, that all comes from water, and to water all returns. And secondly, that the earth is a flat disc which floats upon water.

The first, which is the chief proposition, means that water is the one primal kind of existence and that everything else in the universe is merely a modification of water. Two questions will naturally occur to us. Why did Thales choose water as the first principle? And by what process does water, in his opinion, come to be changed into other things; how was the universe formed out of water? We cannot answer either of these questions with certainty. Aristotle says that Thales "probably derived his opinion from observing that the nutriment of all things is moist, and that even actual heat is generated therefrom, and that animal life is sustained by water, ... and from the fact that the seeds of all things possess a moist nature, and that water is a first principle of all things that are humid." This is very likely the true explanation. But it will be noted that even Aristotle uses the word "probably," and so gives his statement merely as a conjecture. How, in the opinion of Thales, the universe arose out of water, is even more uncertain. Most likely he never asked himself the question, and gave no explanation. At any rate nothing is known on the point.

This being the sum and substance of the teaching of Thales, we may naturally ask why, on account of such a crude and undeveloped idea, he should be given the title of the father of philosophy. Why should philosophy be said to begin here in particular? Now, the significance of Thales is not that his water-philosophy has any value in itself, but that this was the first recorded attempt to explain the universe on naturalistic and scientific principles, without the aid of myths and anthropomorphic gods. Moreover, Thales propounded the problem, and determined the direction and character, of all pre-Socratic philosophy. The fundamental thought of that period was, that under the multiplicity of the world there must be a single ultimate principle. The problem of all philosophers from Thales to Anaxagoras was, what is the nature of that first principle from which all things have issued? Their systems are all attempts to answer this question, and may be classified according to their different replies. Thus Thales asserted that the ultimate reality is water, Anaximander indefinite matter, Anaximenes air, the Pythagoreans number, the Eleatics Being, Heracleitus fire, Empedocles the four elements, Democritus atoms, and so on. The first period is thus essentially cosmological in character, and it was Thales who determined the character. His importance is that he was the first to propound the question, not that he gave any rational reply to it.

We saw in the first chapter, that man is naturally a materialist, and that philosophy is the movement from sensuous to non-sensuous thought. As we should expect, then, philosophy begins in materialism. The first answer to the question, what the ultimate reality is, places the nature of that reality in a sensuous object, water. The other members of the Ionic school, Anaximander, and Anaximenes, are also materialists. And from their time onwards we can trace the gradual rise of thought, with occasional breaks and relapses, from this sensualism of the Ionics, through the semi-sensuous idealism of the Eleatics, to the highest point of pure non-sensuous thought, the idealism of Plato and Aristotle. It is important to keep in mind, then, that the history of philosophy is not a mere chaotic hotch-potch of opinions and theories, succeeding each other without connection or order. It is a logical and historical evolution, each step in which is determined by the last, and advances beyond the last towards a definite goal. The goal, of course, is visible to us, but was not visible to the early thinkers themselves.

Since man begins by looking outwards upon the external world and not inwards upon his own self, this fact too determines the character of the first period of Greek philosophy. It concerns itself solely with nature, with the external world, and only with man as a part of nature. It demands an explanation of nature. And this is the same as saying that it is cosmological. The problems of man, of life, of human destiny, of ethics, are treated by it scantily, or not at all. It is not till the time of the Sophists that the Greek spirit turns inwards upon itself and begins to consider these problems, and with the emergence of that point of view we have passed from the first to the second period of Greek philosophy.

Because the Ionic philosophers were all materialists they are also sometimes called Hylicists, from the Greek hulé which means matter.

Anaximander

The next philosopher of the Ionic school is Anaximander. He was an exceedingly original and audacious thinker. He was probably born about

611 B.C. and died about 547. He was an inhabitant of Miletus, and is said to have been a disciple of Thales. It will be seen, thus, that he was a younger contemporary of Thales. He was born at the time that Thales was flourishing, and was about a generation younger. He was the first Greek to write a philosophic treatise, which however has been unfortunately lost. He was eminent for his astronomical and geographical knowledge, and in this connection was the first to construct a map. Details of his life are not known.

Now Thales had made the ultimate principle of the universe, water. Anaximander agrees with Thales that the ultimate principle of things is material, but he does not name it water, does not in fact believe that it is any particular kind of matter. It is rather a formless, indefinite, and absolutely featureless matter in general. Matter, as we know it, is always some particular kind of matter. It must be iron, brass, water, air, or other such. The difference between the different kinds of matter is qualitative, that is to say, we know that air is air because it has the qualities of air and differs from iron because iron has the qualities of iron, and so on. The primeval matter of Anaximander is just matter not yet sundered into the different kinds of matter. It is therefore formless and characterless. And as it is thus indeterminate in quality, so it is illimitable in quantity. Anaximander believed that this matter stretches out to infinity through space. The reason he gave for this opinion was, that if there were a limited amount of matter it would long ago have been used up in the creation and destruction of the "innumerable worlds." Hence he called it "the boundless." In regard to these "innumerable worlds," the traditional opinion about Anaximander was that he believed these worlds to succeed each other in time, and that first a world was created, developed, and was destroyed, then another world arose, was developed and destroyed, and that this periodic revolution of worlds went on for ever. Professor Burnet, however, is of opinion that the "innumerable worlds" of Anaximander were not necessarily successive but rather simultaneously existing worlds. According to this view there may be any number of worlds existing at the same time. But, even so, it is still true that these worlds were not everlasting, but began, developed and decayed, giving place in due time to other worlds.

How, now, have these various worlds been formed out of the formless, indefinite, indeterminate matter of Anaximander? On this question Anaximander is vague and has nothing very definite to put forward. Indeterminate matter by a vaguely conceived process separates itself into "the hot" and "the cold." The cold is moist or damp. This cold and moist matter becomes the earth, in the centre of the universe. The hot matter collects into a sphere of fire surrounding the earth. The earth in the centre was originally fluid. The heat of the surrounding sphere caused the waters of the earth progressively to evaporate giving rise to the envelope of air which surrounds the earth. For the early Greeks regarded the air and vapour as the same thing. As this air or vapour expanded under the action of heat it burst the outside hot sphere of fire into a series of enormous "wheel-shaped husks," resembling cart wheels, which encircle the earth. You may naturally ask how it is that if these are composed of fire we do not see them continually glowing. Anaximander's answer was that these wheel-shaped husks are encrusted with thick, opaque vapour, which conceals the inner fire from our view. But there are apertures, or pipe-like holes in the vapour-crust, and through these the fire gleams, causing the appearance of the sun, stars, and moon. You will note that the moon was, on this theory, considered to be fiery, and not, as we now know it to be, a cold surface reflecting the sun's light. There were three of these "cart wheels"; the first was that of the sun, furthest away from the earth, nearer to us was that of the moon, and closest of all was that of the fixed stars. The "wheel-shaped husks" containing the heavenly bodies are revolved round the earth by means of currents of air. The earth in the centre was believed by Anaximander to be not spherical but cylindrical. Men live on the top end of this pillar or cylinder.

Anaximander also developed a striking theory about the origin and evolution of living beings. In the beginning the earth was fluid and in the gradual drying up by evaporation of this fluid, living beings were produced from the heat and moisture. In the first instance these beings were of a low order. They gradually evolved into successively higher and higher organisms by means of adaptation to their environment. Man was in the first instance a fish living in the water. The gradual drying up left parts of the earth high and dry, and marine animals migrated to the land, and their fins by adaptation became members fitted for movement on land. The resemblance of this primitive theory to modern theories of evolution is remarkable. It is easy to exaggerate its importance, but it is at any rate clear that Anaximander had, by a happy guess, hit upon the central idea of adaptation of species to their environment.

The teaching of Anaximander exhibits a marked advance beyond the position of Thales. Thales had taught that the first principle of things is water. The formless matter of Anaximander is, philosophically, an advance on this, showing the operation of thought and abstraction. Secondly, Anaximander had definitely attempted to apply this idea, and to derive from it the existent world. Thales had left the question how the primal water developed into a world, entirely unanswered.

Anaximenes

Like the two previous thinkers Anaximenes was an inhabitant of Miletus. He was born about 588 B.C. and died about 524. He wrote a treatise of which a small fragment still remains. He agreed with Thales and Anaximander that the first principle of the universe is material. With Thales too, he looked upon it as a particular kind of matter, not indeterminate matter as taught by Anaximander. Thales had declared it to be water. Anaximenes named air as first principle. This air, like the matter of Anaximander, stretches illimitably through space. Air is constantly in motion and has the power of motion inherent in it and this motion brought about the development of the universe from air. As operating process of this development Anaximenes named the two opposite processes of (1) Rarefaction, (2) Condensation. Rarefaction is the same thing as heat or growing hot, and condensation is identified with growing cold. The air by rarefaction becomes fire, and fire borne aloft upon the air becomes the stars. By the opposite process of condensation, air first becomes clouds and, by further degrees of condensation, becomes successively water, earth, and rocks. The world resolves again in the course of time into the primal air. Anaximenes, like Anaximander, held the theory of "innumerable worlds," and these worlds are, according to the traditional view, successive. But here again Professor Burnet considers that the innumerable worlds may have been co-existent as well as successive. Anaximenes considered the earth to be a flat disc floating upon air.

The origin of the air theory of Anaximenes seems to have been suggested to him by the fact that air in the form of breath is the principle of life.

The teaching of Anaximenes seems at first sight to be a falling off from the position of Anaximander, because he goes back to the position of Thales in favour of a determinate matter as first principle. But in one respect at least there is here an advance upon Anaximander. The latter had been vague as to how formless matter differentiates itself into the world of objects. Anaximenes names the definite processes of rarefaction and condensation. If you believe, as these early physicists did, that every different kind of matter is ultimately one kind of matter, the problem of the differentiation of the qualities of the existent elements arises. For example, if this paper is really composed of air, how do we account for its colour, its hardness, texture, etc. Either these qualities must be originally in the primal air, or not. If the qualities existed in it then it was not really one homogeneous matter like air, but must have been simply a mixture of different kinds of matter. If not, how do these properties arise? How can this air which has not in it the qualities of things we see, develop them? The simplest way of getting out of the difficulty is to found quality upon quantity, and to explain the former by the amount or quantity, more or less, of matter existent in the same volume. This is precisely what is meant by rarefaction and condensation. Condensation would result in compressing more matter into the same volume. Rarefaction would give rise to the opposite process. Great compression of air, a great amount of it in a small space, might account for the qualities, say, of earth and stones, for example, their heaviness, hardness, colour, etc.

Hence Anaximenes was to some extent a more logical and definite thinker than Anaximander, but cannot compare with him in audacity and originality of thought.

Other Ionic Thinkers

We have now considered the three chief thinkers of the Ionic School. Others there were, but they added nothing new to the teaching of these three. They followed either Thales or Anaximenes in stating the first principle of the world either as water or as air. Hippo, for example, followed Thales, and for him the world is composed of water, Idaeus agreed with Anaximenes that it is derived from air. Diogenes of Apollonia is chiefly remarkable for the fact that he lived at a very much later date. He was a contemporary of Anaxagoras, and opposed to the more developed teachings of that philosopher the crude materialism of the Ionic School. Air was by him considered to be the ground of all things.

CHAPTER III

THE PYTHAGOREANS

Not much is known of the life of Pythagoras. Three so-called biographies have come down to us from antiquity, but they were written hundreds of years after the event, and are filled with a tissue of extravagant fancies, and with stories of miracles and wonders worked by Pythagoras. All sorts of fantastic legends seem to have gathered very early around his life, obscuring from us the actual historical details. A few definite facts, however, are known. He was born somewhere between 580 and 570 B.C. at Samos, and about middle age he migrated to Crotona in South Italy. According to legend, before he arrived in South Italy he had travelled extensively in Egypt and other countries of the East. There is, however, no historical evidence of this. There is nothing in itself improbable in the belief that Pythagoras made these travels, but it cannot be accepted as proved for lack of evidence. The legend is really founded simply upon the oriental flavour of his doctrines. In middle age he arrived in South Italy and settled at Crotona. There he founded the Pythagorean Society and lived for many years at the head of it. His later life, the date and manner of his death, are not certainly known.

Now it is important to note that the Pythagorean Society was not primarily a school of philosophy at all. It was really a religious and moral Order, a Society of religious reformers. The Pythagoreans were closely associated with the Orphic Sect, and took from it the belief in the transmigration of souls, including transmigration of human souls into animals. They also taught the doctrine of the "wheel of things," and the necessity of obtaining "release" from it, by which one could escape from the weary round of reincarnate lives. Thus they shared with the Orphic religious Sect the principle of reincarnation. The Orphic Sect believed that "release" from the wheel of life was to be obtained by religious ceremonial and ritual. The Pythagoreans had a similar ritual, but they added to this the belief that intellectual pursuits, the cultivation of science and philosophy, and, in general, the intellectual contemplation of the ultimate things of the universe would be of great help towards the "release" of the soul. From this arose the tendency to develop science and philosophy. Gradually their philosophy attained a semi-independence from their religious rites which justifies us in regarding it definitely as philosophy.

The Pythagorean ethical views were rigorous and ascetic in character. They insisted upon the utmost purity of life in the members of the Order. Abstinence from flesh was insisted upon, although this was apparently a late development. We know that Pythagoras himself was not a total abstainer from flesh. They forbade the eating of beans. They wore a garb peculiar to themselves. The body, they taught, is the prison or tomb of the soul. They thought that one must not attempt to obtain "release" by suicide, because "man is the property of God," the chattel of God. They were not politicians in the modern sense, but their procedure in practice amounted to the greatest possible interference in politics. It appears that the Pythagoreans attempted to impose their ordinances upon the ordinary citizens of Crotona. They aimed at the supersession of the State by their own Order and they did actually capture the government of Crotona for a short period. This led to attacks on the Order, and the persecution of its members. When the plain citizen of Crotona was told not to eat beans, and that under no circumstances could he eat his own dog, this was too much. A general persecution occurred. The meeting place of the Pythagoreans was burnt to the ground, the Society was scattered, and its members killed or driven away. This occurred between the years 440 and 430 B.C. Some years later the Society revived and continued its activities, but we do not hear much of it after the fourth century B.C.

It was largely a mystical society. The Pythagoreans developed their own ritual, ceremonial and mysteries. This love of mystery, and their general character as miracle-mongers, largely account for the legends which grew up around the life of Pythagoras himself. Their scientific activities were also considerable. They enforced moral self-control. They cultivated the arts and crafts, gymnastics, music, medicine, and mathematics. The development of mathematics in early Greece was largely the work of the Pythagoreans. Pythagoras is said to have discovered the 47th Proposition of Euclid, and to have sacrificed an ox in honour thereof. And there is good reason to believe that practically the whole of the substance of the First Book of Euclid is the work of Pythagoras.

Turning now to their philosophical teaching, the first thing that we have to understand is that we cannot speak of the philosophy of Pythagoras, but only of the philosophy of the Pythagoreans. For it is not known what share Pythagoras had in this philosophy or what share was contributed by his successors. Now we recognize objects in the universe by means of their qualities. But the majority of these qualities are not universal in their scope; some things possess some qualities; others possess others. A leaf, for example, is green, but not all things are green. Some things have no colour at all. The same is true of tastes and smells. Some things are sweet; some bitter. But there is one quality in things which is absolutely universal in its scope, which applies to everything in the universe--corporeal or incorporeal. All things are numerable, and can be counted. Moreover, it is impossible to conceive a universe in which number is not to be found. You could easily imagine a universe in which there is no colour, or no sweet taste, or a universe in which nothing possesses weight. But you cannot imagine a universe in which there is no number. This is an inconceivable thought. Upon these grounds we should be justified in concluding that number is an extremely important aspect of things, and forms a fundamental pad of the framework of the world. And it is upon this aspect of things that the Pythagoreans laid emphasis.

They drew attention to proportion, order, and harmony as the dominant notes of the universe. Now when we examine the ideas of proportion, order, and harmony, we shall see that they are closely connected with number. Proportion, for example, must necessarily be expressible by the relation of one number to another. Similarly order is measurable by numbers. When we say that the ranks of a regiment exhibit order, we mean that they are arranged in such a way that the soldiers stand at certain regular distances from each other, and these distances are measurable by numbers of feet or inches. Lastly, consider the idea of harmony. If, in modern times, we were to say that the universe is a harmonious whole, we should understand that we are merely using a metaphor from music. But the Pythagoreans lived in an age when men were not practised in thought, and they confused cosmical harmony with musical harmony. They thought that the two things were the same. Now musical harmony is founded upon numbers, and the Pythagoreans were the first to discover this. The difference of notes is due to the different numbers of vibrations of the sounding instrument. The musical intervals are likewise based upon numerical proportions. So that since, for the Pythagoreans, the universe is a musical harmony, it follows that the essential character of the universe is number. The study of mathematics confirmed the Pythagoreans in this idea. Arithmetic is the science of numbers, and all other mathematical sciences are ultimately reducible to numbers. For instance, in geometry, angles are measured by the number of degrees.

Now, as already pointed out, considering all these facts, we might well be justified in concluding that number is a very important aspect of the universe, and is fundamental in it. But the Pythagoreans went much further than this. They drew what seems to us the extraordinary conclusion that the world is made of numbers. At this point, then, we reach the heart of the Pythagorean philosophy. Just as Thales had said that the ultimate reality, the first principle of which things are composed, is water, so now the Pythagoreans teach that the first principle of things is number. Number is the world-ground, the stuff out of which the universe is made.

In the detailed application of this principle to the world of things we have a conglomeration of extraordinary fancies and extravagances. In the first place, all numbers arise out of the unit. This is the prime number, every other number being simply so many units. The unit then is the first in the order of things in the universe. Again, numbers are divided into odd and even. The universe, said the Pythagoreans, is composed of pairs of opposites and contradictories, and the fundamental character of these opposites is that they are composed of the odd and even. The odd and even, moreover, they identified with the limited and the unlimited respectively. How this identification was made seems somewhat doubtful. But it is clearly connected with the theory of bipartition. An even number can be divided by two and therefore it does not set a limit to bipartition.

Hence it is unlimited. An odd number cannot be divided by two, and therefore it sets a limit to bipartition. The limited and the unlimited become therefore the ultimate principles of the universe. The Limit is identified with the unit, and this again with the central fire of the universe. The Limit is first formed and proceeds to draw more and more of the unlimited towards itself, and to limit it. Becoming limited, it becomes a definite "something," a thing. So the formation of the world of things proceeds. The Pythagoreans drew up a list of ten opposites of which the universe is composed. They are (1) Limited and unlimited, (2) odd and even, (3) one and many, (4) right and left, (5) masculine and feminine, (6) rest and motion, (7) straight and crooked, (8) light and darkness, (9) good and evil, (10) square and oblong.

With the further development of the number-theory Pythagoreanism becomes entirely arbitrary and without principle. We hear, for example, that 1 is the point, 2 is the line, 3 is the plane, 4 is the solid, 5 physical qualities, 6 animation, 7 intelligence, health, love, wisdom. There is no principle in all this. Identification of the different numbers with different things can only be left to the whim and fancy of the individual. The Pythagoreans disagreed among themselves as to what number is to be assigned to what thing. For example, justice, they said, is that which returns equal for equal. If I do a man an injury, justice ordains that injury should be done to me, thus giving equal for equal. Justice must, therefore, be a number which returns equal for equal. Now the only numbers which do this are square numbers. Four equals two into two, and so returns equal for equal. Four, then, must be justice. But nine is equally the square of three. Hence other Pythagoreans identified justice with nine.

According to Philolaus, one of the most prominent Pythagoreans, the quality of matter depends upon the number of sides of its smallest particles. Of the five regular solids, three were known to the Pythagoreans. That matter whose smallest particles are regular tetrahedra, said Philolaus, is fire. Similarly earth is composed of cubes, and the universe is identified with the dodecahedron. This idea was developed further by Plato in the

"Timaeus," where we find all the five regular solids brought into the theory.

The central fire, already mentioned as identified with the unit, is a characteristic doctrine of the Pythagoreans. Up to this time it had been believed that the earth is the centre of the universe, and that everything revolves round it. But with the Pythagoreans the earth revolves round the central fire. One feels inclined at once to identify this with the sun. But this is not correct. The sun, like the earth, revolves round the central fire. We do not see the central fire because that side of the earth on which we live is perpetually turned away from it. This involves the theory that the earth revolves round the central fire in the same period that it takes to rotate upon its axis. The Pythagoreans were the first to see that the earth is itself one of the planets, and to shake themselves free from the geocentric hypothesis. Round the central fire, sometimes mystically called "the Hearth of the Universe," revolve ten bodies. First is the "counter-earth," a non-existent body invented by the Pythagoreans, next comes the earth, then the sun, the moon, the five planets, and lastly the heaven of the fixed stars. This curious system might have borne fruit in astronomy. That it did not do so was largely due to the influence of Aristotle, who discountenanced the theory, and insisted that the earth is the centre of the universe. But in the end the Pythagorean view won the day. We know that Copernicus derived the suggestion of his heliocentric hypothesis from the Pythagoreans.

The Pythagoreans also taught "The Great Year," probably a period of 10,000 years, in which the world comes into being and passes away, going in each such period through the same evolution down to the smallest details.

There is little to be said by way of criticism of the Pythagorean system. It is entirely crude philosophy. The application of the number theory issues in a barren and futile arithmetical mysticism. Hegel's words in this connection are instructive:--

"We may certainly," he says, "feel ourselves prompted to associate the most general characteristics of thought with the first numbers: saying one is the simple and immediate, two is difference and mediation, and three the unity of both these. Such associations however are purely external; there is nothing in the mere numbers to make them express these definite thoughts. With every step in this method, the more arbitrary grows the association of definite numbers with definite thoughts ... To attach, as do some secret societies of modern times, importance to all sorts of numbers and figures is, to some extent an innocent amusement, but it is also a sign of deficiency of intellectual resource. These numbers, it is said, conceal a profound meaning, and suggest a deal to think about. But the point in philosophy is not what you may think but what you do think; and the genuine air of thought is to be sought in thought itself and not in arbitrarily selected symbols."

CHAPTER IV

THE ELEATICS

The Eleatics are so called because the seat of their school was at Elea, a town in South Italy, and Parmenides and Zeno, the two chief representatives of the school, were both citizens of Elea. So far we have been dealing with crude systems of thought in which only the germs of philosophic thinking can be dimly discerned. Now, however, with the Eleatics we step out definitely for the first time upon the platform of philosophy. Eleaticism is the first true philosophy. In it there emerges the first factor of the truth, however poor, meagre, and inadequate. For philosophy is not, as many persons suppose, simply a collection of freak speculations, which we may study in historical order, but at the end of which, God alone knows which we ought to believe. On the contrary, the history of philosophy presents a definite line of evolution. The truth unfolds itself gradually in time.

Xenophanes

The reputed founder of the Eleatic School was Xenophanes. It is, however, doubtful whether Xenophanes ever went to Elea. Moreover, he belongs more properly to the history of religion than to the history of philosophy. The real creator of the Eleatic School was Parmenides. But Parmenides seized upon certain germs of thought latent in Xenophanes and transmuted them into philosophic principles. We have, therefore, in the first instance, to say something of Xenophanes. He was born about the year 576 B.C., at Colophon in Ionia. His long life was spent in wandering up and down the cities of Hellas, as a poet and minstrel, singing songs at banquets and festivals. Whether, as sometimes stated; he finally settled at Elea is a matter of doubt, but we know definitely that at the advanced age of ninety-two he was still wandering about Greece. His philosophy, such as it is, is expressed in poems. He did not, however, write philosophical poems, but rather elegies and satires upon various subjects, only incidentally expressing his religious views therein. Fragments of these poems have come down to us.

Xenophanes is the originator of the quarrel between philosophy and religion. He attacked the popular religious notions of the Greeks with a view to founding a purer and nobler conception of Deity. Popular Greek religion consisted of a belief in a number of gods who were conceived very much as in the form of human beings. Xenophanes attacks this conception of God as possessing human form. It is absurd, he says, to suppose that the gods wander about from place to place, as represented in the Greek legends. It is absurd to suppose that the gods had a beginning. It is disgraceful to impute to them stories of fraud, adultery, theft and deceit. And Xenophanes inveighs against Homer and Hesiod for disseminating these degrading conceptions of the Deity. He argues, too, against the polytheistic notion of a plurality of gods. That which is divine can only be one. There can only be one best. Therefore, God is to be conceived as one. And this God is comparable to mortals neither in bodily form nor understanding. He is "all eye, all ear, all thought." It is he "who, without trouble, by his thought governs all things." But it would be a mistake to suppose that Xenophanes thought of this God as a being external to the world, governing it from the outside, as a general governs his soldiers. On the contrary, Xenophanes identified God with the world. The world is God, a sentient being, though without organs of sense. Looking out into the wide heavens, he said, "The One is God." The thought of Xenophanes is therefore more properly described as pantheism than as monotheism. God is unchangeable, immutable, undivided, unmoved, passionless, undisturbed. Xenophanes appears, thus, rather as a religious reformer than as a philosopher. Nevertheless, inasmuch as he was the first to enunciate the proposition "All is one," he takes his place in philosophy. It was upon this thought that Parmenides built the foundations of the Eleatic philosophy.

Certain other opinions of Xenophanes have been preserved. He observed fossils, and found shells inland, and the forms of fish and sea-weed embedded in the rocks in the quarries of Syracuse and elsewhere. From these he concluded that the earth had risen out of the sea and would again partially sink into it. Then the human race would be destroyed. But the earth would again rise from the sea and the human race would again be renewed. He believed that the sun and stars were burning masses of vapour. The sun, he thought, does not revolve round the earth. It goes on in a straight line, and disappears in the remote distance in the evening. It is not the same sun which rises the next morning. Every day a new sun is formed out of the vapours of the sea. This idea is connected with his general attitude towards the popular religion. His motive was to show that the sun and stars are not divine beings, but like other beings, ephemeral. Xenophanes also ridiculed the Pythagoreans, especially their doctrine of re-incarnation.

Parmenides

Parmenides was born about 514 B.C. at Elea. Not much is known of his life. He was in his early youth a Pythagorean, but recanted that philosophy and formulated a philosophy of his own. He was greatly revered in antiquity both for the depth of his intellect, and the sublimity and nobility of his character. Plato refers to him always with reverence. His philosophy is comprised in a philosophic didactic poem which is divided into two parts. The first part expounds his own philosophy and is called "the way of truth." The second part describes the false opinions current in his day and is called "the way of opinion."

The reflection of Parmenides takes its rise from observation of the transitoriness and changeableness of things. The world, as we know it, is a world of change and mutation. All things arise and pass away. Nothing is permanent, nothing stands. One moment it is, another moment it is not. It is as true to say of anything, that it is not, as that it is. The truth of things cannot lie here, for no knowledge of that which is constantly changing is possible. Hence the thought of Parmenides becomes the effort to find the eternal amid the shifting, the abiding and everlasting amid the change and mutation of things. And there arises in this way the antithesis between Being and not-being. The absolutely real is Being. Not-being is the unreal. Not-being is not at all. And this not-being he identifies with becoming, with the world of shifting and changing things, the world which is known to us by the senses. The world of sense is unreal, illusory, a mere appearance. It is not-being. Only Being truly is. As Thales designated water the one reality, as the Pythagoreans named number, so now for Parmenides the sole reality, the first principle of things, is Being, wholly unmixed with not-being, wholly excludent of all becoming. The character of Being he describes, for the most part, in a series of negatives. There is in it no change, it is absolutely unbecome and imperishable. It has neither beginning nor end, neither arising nor passing away. If Being began, it must have arisen either from Being or from not-being. But for Being to arise out of Being, that is not a beginning, and for Being to arise out of not-being is impossible, since there is then no reason why it should arise later rather than sooner. Being cannot come out of not-being, nor something out of nothing. Ex nihilo nihil fit. This is the fundamental thought of Parmenides. Moreover, we cannot say of Being that it was, that it is, that it will be. There is for it no past, no present, and no future. It is rather eternally and timelessly present. It is undivided and indivisible. For anything to be divided it must be divided by something other than itself. But there is nothing other than Being; there is no not-being. Therefore there is nothing by which Being can be divided. Hence it is indivisible. It is unmoved and undisturbed, for motion and disturbance are forms of becoming, and all becoming is excluded from Being. It is absolutely self-identical. It does not arise from anything other than itself. It does not pass into anything other than itself. It has its whole being in itself. It does not depend upon anything else for its being and reality. It does not pass over into otherness; it remains, steadfast, and abiding in itself. Of positive character Being has nothing. Its sole character is simply its being. It cannot be said that it is this or that; it cannot be said that it has this or that quality, that it is here or there, then or now. It simply is. Its only quality is, so to speak, "isness."

But in Parmenides there emerges for the first time a distinction of fundamental importance in philosophy, the distinction between Sense and Reason. The world of falsity and appearance, of becoming, of not-being, this is, says Parmenides, the world which is presented to us by the senses. True and veritable Being is known to us only by reason, by thought. The senses therefore, are, for Parmenides, the sources of all illusion and error. Truth lies only in reason. This is exceedingly important, because this,that truth lies in reason and not in the world of sense, is the fundamental position of idealism.

The doctrine of Being, just described, occupies the first part of the poem of Parmenides. The second part is the way of false opinion. But whether Parmenides is here simply giving an account of the false philosophies of his day, (and in doing this there does not seem much point,) or whether he was, with total inconsistency, attempting, in a cosmological theory of his own, to explain the origin of that world of appearance and illusion, whose very being he has, in the first part of the poem, denied--this does not seem to be clear. The theory here propounded, at any rate, is that the sense-world is composed of the two opposites, the hot and the cold, or light and darkness. The more hot there is, the more life, the more reality; the more cold, the more unreality and death.

What position, now, are we to assign to Parmenides in philosophy? How are we to characterize his system? Such writers as Hegel, Erdmann, and Schwegler, have always interpreted his philosophy in an idealistic sense. Professor Burnet, however, takes the opposite view. To quote his own words: "Parmenides is not, as some have said, the father of idealism. On the contrary, all materialism depends upon his view." Now if we cannot say whether Parmenides was a materialist or an idealist, we cannot be said to understand much about his philosophy. The question is therefore of cardinal importance. Let us see, in the first place, upon what grounds the materialistic interpretation of Parmenides is based. It is based upon a fact which I have so far not mentioned, leaving it for explanation at this moment. Parmenides said that Being, which is for him the ultimate reality, occupies space, is finite, and is spherical or globe-shaped. Now that which occupies space, and has shape, is matter. The ultimate reality of things, therefore, is conceived by Parmenides as material, and this, of course, is the cardinal thesis of materialism. This interpretation of Parmenides is further emphasized in the disagreement between himself and Melissus, as to whether Being is finite or infinite. Melissus was a younger adherent of the Eleatic School, whose chief interest lies in his views on this question. His philosophical position in general is the same as that of Parmenides. But on this point they differed. Parmenides asserted that Being is globe-shaped, and therefore finite. Now it was an essential part of the doctrine of Parmenides that empty space is non-existent. Empty space is an existent non-existence. This is self-contradictory, and for Parmenides, therefore, empty space is simply not-being. There are, for example, no interstices, or empty spaces between the particles of matter. Being is "the full," that is, full space with no mixture of empty space in it. Now Melissus agreed with Parmenides that there is no such thing as empty space; and he pointed out, that if Being is globe-shaped, it must be bounded on the outside by empty space. And as this is impossible, it cannot be true that Being is globe-shaped, or finite, but must, on the contrary, extend illimitably through space. This makes it quite clear that Parmenides, Melissus, and the Eleatics generally, did regard Being as, in some sense, material.

Now, however, let us turn to the other side of the picture. What ground is there for regarding Parmenides as an idealist? In the first place, we may say that his ultimate principle, Being, whatever he may have thought of it, is not in fact material, but is essentially an abstract thought, a concept. Being is not here, it is not there. It is not in any place or time. It is not to be found by the senses. It is to be found only in reason. We form the idea of Being by the process of abstraction. For example, we see this desk. Our entire knowledge of the desk consists in our knowledge of its qualities. It is square, brown, hard, odourless, etc. Now suppose we successively strip off these qualities in thought--its colour, its size, its shape. We shall ultimately be left with nothing at all except its mere being. We can no longer say of it that it is hard, square, etc. We can only say "it is." As Parmenides said, Being is not divisible, movable; it is not here nor there, then nor now. It simply "is." This is the Eleatic notion of Being, and it is a pure concept. It may be compared to such an idea as "whiteness." We cannot see "whiteness." We see white things, but not "whiteness" itself. What, then, is "whiteness"? It is a concept, that is to say, not a particular thing, but a general idea, which we form by abstraction, by considering the quality which all white things have in common, and neglecting the qualities in which they differ. Just so, if we consider the common character of all objects in the universe, and neglect their differences, we shall find that what they all have in common is simply "being." Being then is a general idea, or concept. It is a thought, and not a thing. Parmenides, therefore, actually placed the absolute reality of things in an idea, in a thought, though he may have conceived it in a material and sensuous way. Now the cardinal thesis of idealism is precisely this, that the absolute reality, of which the world is a manifestation, consists in thought, in concepts. Parmenides, on this view, was an idealist.

Moreover, Parmenides has clearly made the distinction between sense and reason. True Being is not known to the senses, but only to reason, and this distinction is an essential feature of all idealism. Materialism is precisely the view that reality is to be found in the world of sense. But the proposition of Parmenides is the exact opposite of this, namely, that reality is to be found only in reason. Again, there begins to appear for the first time in Parmenides the distinction between reality and appearance. Parmenides, of course, would not have used these terms, which have been adopted in modern times. But the thought which they express is unmistakably there. This outward world, the world of sense, he proclaims to be illusion and appearance. Reality is something which lies behind, and is invisible to the senses. Now the very essence of materialism is that this material world, this world of sense, is the real world. Idealism is the doctrine that the sense-world is an appearance. How then can Parmenides be called a materialist?

How are we to reconcile these two conflicting views of Parmenides? I think the truth is that these two contradictories lie side by side in Parmenides unreconciled, and still mutually contradicting each other. Parmenides himself did not see the contradiction. If we emphasize the one side, then Parmenides was a materialist. If we emphasize the other side, then he is to be interpreted as an idealist. In point of fact, in the history of Greek philosophy, both these sides of Parmenides were successively emphasized. He became the father both of materialism and of idealism. His immediate successors, Empedocles and Democritus, seized upon the materialistic aspect of his thought, and developed it. The essential thought of Parmenides was that Being cannot arise from not-being, and that Being neither arises nor passes away. If we apply this idea to matter we get what in modern times is called the doctrine of the "indestructibility of matter." Matter has no beginning and no end. The apparent arising and passing away of things is simply the aggregation and separation of particles of matter which, in themselves, are indestructible. This is precisely the position of Democritus. And his doctrine, therefore, is a materialistic rendering of the main thought of Parmenides that Being cannot arise from not-being or pass into not-being.

It was not till the time of Plato that the idealistic aspect of the Parmenidean doctrine was developed. It was the genius of Plato which seized upon the germs of idealism in Parmenides and developed them. Plato was deeply influenced by Parmenides. His main doctrine was that the reality of the world is to be found in thought, in concepts, in what is called "the Idea." And he identified the Idea with the Being of Parmenides.

But still, it may be asked, which is the true view of Parmenides? Which is the historical Parmenides? Was not Plato in interpreting him idealistically reading his own thought into Parmenides? Are not we, if we interpret him as an idealist, reading into him later ideas? In one sense this is perfectly true. It is clear from what Parmenides himself said that he regarded the ultimate reality of things as material. It would be a complete mistake to attribute to him a fully developed and consistent system of idealism. If you had told Parmenides that he was an idealist, he would not have understood you. The distinction between materialism and idealism was not then developed. If you had told him, moreover, that Being is a concept, he would not have understood you, because the theory of concepts was not developed until the time of Socrates and Plato. Now it is the function of historical criticism to insist upon this, to see that later thought is not attributed to Parmenides. But if this is the function of historical scholarship, it is equally the function of philosophic insight to seize upon the germs of a higher thought amid the confused thinking of Parmenides, to see what he was groping for, to see clearly what he saw only vaguely and dimly, to make explicit what in him was merely implicit, to exhibit the true inwardness of his teaching, to separate what is valuable and essential in it from what is worthless and accidental. And I say that in this sense the true and essential meaning of Parmenides is his idealism. I said in the first chapter that philosophy is the movement from sensuous to non-sensuous thought. I said that it is only with the utmost difficulty that this movement occurs. And I said that even the greatest philosophers have sometimes failed herein. In Parmenides we have the first example of this. He began by propounding the truth that Being is the essential reality, and Being, as we saw, is a concept. But Parmenides was a pioneer. He trod upon unbroken ground. He had not behind him, as we have, a long line of idealistic thinkers to guide him. So he could not maintain this first non-sensuous thought. He could not resist the temptation to frame for himself a mental image, a picture, of Being. Now all mental images and pictures are framed out of materials supplied to us by the senses. Hence it comes about that Parmenides pictured Being as a globe-shaped something occupying space. But this is not the truth of Parmenides. This is simply his failure to realise and understand his own principle, and to think his own thought. It is true that his immediate successors, Empedocles and Democritus, seized upon this, and built their philosophies upon it. But in doing so they were building upon the darkness of Parmenides, upon his dimness of vision, upon his inability to grapple with his own idea. It was Plato who built upon the light of Parmenides.

Zeno

The third and last important thinker of the Eleatic School is Zeno who, like Parmenides, was a man of Elea. His birth is placed about 489 B.C. He composed a prose treatise in which he developed his philosophy. Zeno's contribution to Eleaticism is, in a sense, entirely negative. He did not add anything positive to the teachings of Parmenides. He supports Parmenides in the doctrine of Being. But it is not the conclusions of Zeno that are novel, it is rather the reasons which he gave for them. In attempting to support the Parmenidean doctrine from a new point of view he developed certain ideas about the ultimate character of space and time which have since been of the utmost importance in philosophy. Parmenides had taught that the world of sense is illusory and false. The essentials of that world are two--

multiplicity and change. True Being is absolutely one; there is in it no plurality or multiplicity. Being, moreover, is absolutely static and unchangeable. There is in it no motion. Multiplicity and motion are the two characteristics of the false world of sense. Against multiplicity and motion, therefore, Zeno directed his arguments, and attempted indirectly to support the conclusions of Parmenides by showing that multiplicity and motion are impossible. He attempted to force multiplicity and motion to refute themselves by showing that, if we assume them as real, contradictory propositions follow from that assumption. Two propositions which contradict each other cannot both be true. Therefore the assumptions from which both follow, namely, multiplicity and motion, cannot be real things.

Zeno's arguments against multiplicity.

(1) If the many is, it must be both infinitely small and infinitely large. The many must be infinitely small. For it is composed of units. This is what we mean by saying that it is many. It is many parts or units. These units must be indivisible. For if they are further divisible, then they are not units. Since they are indivisible they can have no magnitude, for that which has magnitude is divisible. The many, therefore, is composed of units which have no magnitude. But if none of the parts of the many have magnitude, the many as a whole has none. Therefore, the many is infinitely small. But the many must also be infinitely large. For the many has magnitude, and as such, is divisible into parts. These parts still have magnitude, and are therefore further divisible. However far we proceed with the division the parts still have magnitude and are still divisible. Hence the many is divisible ad infinitum. It must therefore be composed of an infinite number of parts, each having magnitude. But the smallest magnitude, multiplied by infinity, becomes an infinite magnitude. Therefore the many is infinitely large. (2) The many must be, in number, both limited and unlimited. It must be limited because it is just as many as it is, no more, no less. It is, therefore, a definite number. But a definite number is a finite or limited number. But the many must be also unlimited in number. For it is infinitely divisible, or composed of an infinite number of parts.

Zeno's arguments against motion.

(1) In order to travel a distance, a body must first travel half the distance. There remains half left for it still to travel. It must then travel half the remaining distance. There is still a remainder. This progress proceeds infinitely, but there is always a remainder untravelled. Therefore, it is impossible for a body to travel from one point to another. It can never arrive. (2) Achilles and the tortoise run a race. If the tortoise is given a start, Achilles can never catch it up. For, in the first place, he must run to the point from which the tortoise started. When he gets there, the tortoise will have gone to a point further on. Achilles must then run to that point, and finds then that the tortoise has reached a third point. This will go on for ever, the distance between them continually diminishing, but never being wholly wiped out. Achilles will never catch up the tortoise. (3) This is the story of the flying arrow. An object cannot be in two places at the same time. Therefore, at any particular moment in its flight the arrow is in one place and not in two. But to be in one place is to be at rest. Therefore in each and every moment of its flight it is at rest. It is thus at rest throughout. Motion is impossible.

This type of argument is, in modern times, called "antinomy." An antinomy is a proof that, since two contradictory propositions equally follow from a given assumption, that assumption must be false. Zeno is also called by Aristotle the inventor of dialectic. Dialectic originally meant simply discussion, but it has come to be a technical term in philosophy, and is used for that type of reasoning which seeks to develop the truth by making the false refute and contradict itself. The conception of dialectic is especially important in Zeno, Plato, Kant, and Hegel.

All the arguments which Zeno uses against multiplicity and motion are in reality merely variations of one argument. That argument is as follows. It applies equally to space, to time, or to anything which can be quantitatively measured. For simplicity we will consider it only in its spatial significance. Any quantity of space, say the space enclosed within a circle, must either be composed of ultimate indivisible units, or it must be divisible ad infinitum. If it is composed of indivisible units, these must have magnitude, and we are faced with the contradiction of a magnitude which cannot be divided. If it is divisible ad infinitum, we are faced with the contradiction of supposing that an infinite number of parts can be added up and make a finite sum-total. It is thus a great mistake to suppose that Zeno's stories of Achilles and the tortoise, and of the flying arrow, are merely childish puzzles. On the contrary, Zeno was the first, by means of these stories, to bring to light the essential contradictions which lie in our ideas of space and time, and thus to set an important problem for all subsequent philosophy.

All Zeno's arguments are based upon the one argument described above, which may be called the antinomy of infinite divisibility. For example, the story of the flying arrow. At any moment of its flight, says Zeno, it must be in one place, because it cannot be in two places at the same moment. This depends upon the view of time as being infinitely divisible. It is only in an infinitesimal moment, an absolute moment having no duration, that the arrow is at rest. This, however, is not the only antinomy which we find in our conceptions of space and time. Every mathematician is acquainted with the contradictions immanent in our ideas of infinity. For example, the familiar proposition that parallel straight lines meet at infinity, is a contradiction. Again, a decreasing geometrical progression can be added up to infinity, the infinite number of its terms adding up in the sum-total to a finite number. The idea of infinite space itself is a contradiction. You can say of it exactly what Zeno said of the many. There must be in existence as much space as there is, no more. But this means that there must be a definite and limited amount of space. Therefore space is finite. On the other hand, it is impossible to conceive a limit to space. Beyond the limit there must be more space. Therefore space is infinite. Zeno himself gave expression to this antinomy in the form of an argument which I have not so far mentioned. He said that everything which exists is in space. Space itself exists, therefore space must be in space. That space must be in another space and so ad infinitum. This of course is merely a quaint way of saying that to conceive a limit to space is impossible.

But to return to the antinomy of infinite divisibility, on which most of Zeno's arguments rest, you will perhaps expect me to say something of the different solutions which have been offered. In the first place, we must not forget Zeno's own solution. He did not propound this contradiction for its own sake, but to support the thesis of Parmenides. His solution is that as multiplicity and motion contain these contradictions, therefore multiplicity and motion cannot be real. Therefore, there is, as Parmenides said, only one Being, with no multiplicity in it, and excludent of all motion and becoming. The solution given by Kant in modern times is essentially similar. According to Kant, these contradictions are immanent in our conceptions of space and time, and since time and space involve these contradictions it follows that they are not real beings, but appearances, mere phenomena. Space and time do not belong to things as they are in themselves, but rather to our way of looking at things. They are forms of our perception. It is our minds which impose space and time upon objects, and not objects which impose space and time upon our minds. Further, Kant drew from these contradictions the conclusion that to comprehend the infinite is beyond the capacity of human reason. He attempted to show that, wherever we try to think the infinite, whether the infinitely large or the infinitely small, we fall into irreconcilable contradictions. Therefore, he concluded that human faculties are incapable of apprehending infinity. As might be expected, many thinkers have attempted to solve the problem by denying one or other side of the contradiction, by saying that one or other side does not follow from the premises, that one is true and the other false. David Hume, for example, denied the infinite divisibility of space and time, and declared that they are composed of indivisible units having magnitude. But the difficulty that it is impossible to conceive of units having magnitude which are yet indivisible is not satisfactorily explained by Hume. And in general, it seems that any solution which is to be satisfactory must somehow make room for both sides of the contradiction. It will not do to deny one side or the other, to say that one is false and the other true. A true solution is only possible by rising above the level of the two antagonistic principles and taking them both up to the level of a higher conception, in which both opposites are reconciled.

This was the procedure followed by Hegel in his solution of the problem. Unfortunately his solution cannot be fully understood without some knowledge of his general philosophical principles, on which it wholly depends. I will, however, try to make it as plain as possible. In the first place, Hegel did not go out of his way to solve these antinomies. They appear as mere incidents in the development of his thought. He did not regard them as isolated cases of contradiction which occur in thought, as exceptions to a general rule, which therefore need special explanation. On the contrary, he regarded them, not as exceptions to, but as examples of, the essential character of reason. All thought, all reason, for Hegel, contains immanent contradictions which it first posits and then reconciles in a higher unity, and this particular contradiction of infinite divisibility is reconciled in the higher notion of quantity. The notion of quantity contains two factors, namely the one and the many. Quantity means precisely a many in one, or a one in many. If, for example, we consider a quantity of anything, say a heap of wheat, this is, in the first place, one; it is one whole. Secondly, it is many; for it is composed of many parts. As one it is continuous; as many it is discrete. Now the true notion of quantity is not one, apart from many, nor many apart from one. It is the synthesis of both. It is a many in one. The antinomy we are considering arises from considering one side of the truth in a false abstraction from the other. To conceive unity as not being in itself multiplicity, or multiplicity as not being unity, is a false abstraction. The thought of the one involves the thought of the many, and the thought of the many involves the thought of the one. You cannot have a many without a one, any more than you can have one end of a stick without the other. Now, if we consider anything which is quantitatively measured, such as a straight line, we may consider it, in the first place, as one. In that case it is a continuous indivisible unit. Next we may regard it as many, in which case it falls into parts. Now each of these parts may again be regarded as one, and as such is an indivisible unit; and again each part may be regarded as many, in which case it falls into further parts; and this alternating process may go on for ever. This is the view of the matter which gives rise to the contradictions we have been considering. But it is a false view. It involves the false abstraction of first regarding the many as something that has reality apart from the one, and then regarding the one as something that has reality apart from the many. If you persist in saying that the line is simply one and not many, then there arises the theory of indivisible units. If you persist in saying it is simply many and not one, then it is divisible ad infinitum. But the truth is that it is neither simply many nor simply one; it is a many in one, that is, it is a quantity. Both sides of the contradiction are, therefore, in one sense true, for each is a factor of the truth. But both sides are also false, if and in so far as, each sets itself up as the whole truth.

Critical Remarks on Eleaticism.

The consideration of the meaning of Zeno's doctrine will give us an insight into the essentials of the position of the Eleatics. Zeno said that motion and multiplicity are not real. Now what does this mean? Did Zeno mean to say that when he walked about the streets of Elea, it was not true that he walked about? Did he mean that it was not a fact that he moved from place to place? When I move my arms, did he mean that I am not moving my arms, but that they really remain at rest all the time? If so, we might justly conclude that this philosophy is a mere craze of speculation run mad, or else a joke. But this is not what is meant. The Eleatic position is that though the world of sense, of which multiplicity and motion are essential features, may exist, yet that outward world is not the true Being. They do not deny that the world exists. They do not deny that motion exists or that multiplicity exists. These things no sane man can deny. The existence of motion and multiplicity is, as Hegel says, as sensuously certain as the existence of elephants. Zeno, then, does not deny the existence of the world. What he denies is the truth of existence. What he means is: certainly there is motion and multiplicity; certainly the world is here, is present to our senses, but it is not the true world. It is not reality. It is mere appearance, illusion, an outward show and sham, a hollow mask which hides the real being of things. You may ask what is meant by this distinction between appearance and reality. Is not even an appearance real? It appears. It exists. Even a delusion exists, and is therefore a real thing. So is not the distinction between appearance and reality itself meaningless?

Now all this is perfectly true, but it does not comprehend quite what is meant by the distinction. What is meant is that the objects around us have existence, but not self-existence, not self-substantiality. That is to say, their being is not in themselves, their existence is not grounded in themselves but is grounded in another, and flows from that other. They exist, but they are not independent existences. They are rather beings whose being flows into them from another, which itself is self-existent and self-substantial. They are, therefore, mere appearances of that other, which is the reality. Of course the Eleatics did not speak of appearance and reality in these terms. But this is what they were groping for, and dimly saw.

If we now look back upon the road on which we have travelled from the beginning of Greek philosophy, we shall be able to characterize the direction in which we have been moving. The earliest Greek philosophers, the Ionics, propounded the question, "what is the ultimate principle of things?" and answered it by declaring that the first principle of things is matter. The second Greek School, the Pythagoreans, answered the same question by declaring numbers to be the first principle. The third school, the Eleatics, answered the question by asserting that the first principle of things is Being. Now the universe, as we know it, is both quantitative and qualitative. Quantity and quality are characteristics of every sense-object. These are not, indeed, the only characteristics of the world, but they are the only characteristics which have so far come to light. Now the position of the Ionics was that the ultimate reality is both quantitative and qualitative, that is to say, it is matter, for matter is just what has both quantity and quality. The Pythagoreans abstracted from the quality of things. They stripped off the qualitative aspect from things, and were accordingly left with only quantity as ultimate reality. Quantity is the same as number. Hence the Pythagorean position that the world is made of numbers. The Eleatic philosophy, proceeding one step further in the same direction, abstracted from quantity as well as quality. Whereas the Pythagoreans had denied the qualitative aspect of things, leaving themselves only with the quantitative, the Eleatics denied both quantity and quality, for in denying multiplicity they denied quantity. Therefore they are left with the total abstraction of mere Being which has in it neither dividedness (quantity), nor positive character (quality). The rise from the Ionic to the Eleatic philosophy is therefore essentially a rise from sensuous to pure thinking. The Eleatic Being is a pure abstract thought. The position of the Pythagoreans on the other hand is that of semi-sensuous thought. They form the stepping-stone from the Ionics to the Eleatics.

Now let us consider what of worth there is in this Eleatic principle, and what its defects are. In the first place, it is necessary for us to understand that the Eleatic philosophy is the first monism. A monistic philosophy is a philosophy which attempts to explain the entire universe from one single principle. The opposite of monism is therefore pluralism, which is that kind of philosophy which seeks to explain the universe from many ultimate and equally underived principles. But more particularly and more frequently we speak of the opposite of monism as being dualism, that is to say, the position that there are two ultimate principles of explanation. If, for example, we say that all the good in the universe arises from one source which is good, and that all the evil arises from another source which is evil, and that these sources of good and evil cannot be subordinated one to the other, and that one does not arise out of the other, but both are co-ordinate and equally primeval and independent, that position would be a dualism. All philosophy, which is worthy of the name, seeks, in some sense, a monistic explanation of the universe, and when we find that a system of philosophy breaks down and fails, then we may nearly always be sure its defect will reveal itself as an unreconciled dualism. Such a philosophy will begin with a monistic principle, and will attempt to derive or deduce the entire universe from it, but somewhere or other it comes across something in the world which it cannot bring under that principle. Then it is left with two equally ultimate existences, neither of which can be derived from the other. Thus it breaks out into dualism.

Now the search for a monistic explanation of things is a universal tendency of human thought. Wherever we look in the world of thought, we find that this monistic tendency appears. I have already said that it appears throughout the history of philosophy. It reveals itself, too, very clearly in the history of religion. Religion begins in polytheism, the belief in many gods. From that it passes on to monotheism, the belief in one God, who is the sole author and creator of the universe. In Hindu thought we find the same thing. Hindu thought is based upon the principle that "All is one." Everything in the world is derived from one ultimate being, Brahman. But not only is this monistic tendency traceable in religion and philosophy; it is also traceable in science. The progress of scientific explanation is essentially a progress towards monism. In the first place, the explanation of isolated facts consists always in assigning causes for them. Suppose there is a strange noise in your room at night. You say it is explained when you find that it is due to the falling of a book or the scuttling of a rat across the floor. The noise is thus explained by assigning a cause for it. But this simply means that you have robbed it of its isolated and exceptional position, and reduced it to the position of an example of a general law. When the water freezes in your jug, you say that the cause of this is the cold. It is an example of the law that whenever the cold reaches a certain degree, then, other things being equal, water solidifies. But to assign causes in this way is not really to explain anything. It does not give any reason for an event happening. You cannot see any reason why water should solidify in the cold. It merely tells us that the event is not exceptional, but is an example of what always happens. It reduces the isolated event to a case of a general law, which "explains," not merely this one event, but possibly millions of events. It is not merely that cold solidifies the water in your jug. It equally solidifies the water in everybody's jug. The same law "explains" all these, and likewise "explains" icebergs and the polar caps on the earth and the planet Mars. In fact scientific explanation means the reduction of millions of facts to one principle. But science does not stop here. It seeks further to explain the laws themselves, and its method is to reduce the many laws to one higher and more general law. A familiar example of this is the explanation of Kepler's laws of the planetary motions. Kepler laid down three such laws. The first was that planets move in elliptical orbits with the sun in one focus. The second was that planets describe equal areas in equal times. The third was a rather more complicated law. Kepler knew these laws from observation, but he could not explain them. They were explained by Newton's discovery of the law of gravitation. Newton proved that Kepler's three laws could be mathematically deduced from the law of gravitation. In that way Kepler's laws were explained, and not only Kepler's laws, but many other astronomical laws and facts. Thus the explanation of the many isolated facts consists in their reduction to the one law, and the explanation of the many laws consists in their reduction to the one more general law. As knowledge advances, the phenomena of the universe come to be explained by fewer and fewer, and wider and wider, general principles. Obviously the ultimate goal would be the explanation of all things by one principle. I do not mean to say that scientific men have this end consciously in view. But the point is that the monistic tendency is there. What is meant by the explanation is the reduction of all things to one principle.

In philosophy, in religion, and in science, then, we find this monistic tendency of thought. But it might be asked how we know that this universal tendency is right? How do we know that it is not merely a universal error? Is there no logical or philosophical basis for the belief that the ultimate explanation of things must be one? Now this is a subject which takes us far afield from Greek philosophy. The philosophical basis of monism was never thought out till the time of Spinoza. So we cannot go into it at length here. But, quite shortly, the question is--Is there any reason for believing that the ultimate explanation of things must be one? Now if we are to explain the universe, two conditions must be fulfilled. In the first place, the ultimate reality by which we attempt to explain everything must explain all the other things in the world. It must be possible to deduce the whole world from it. Secondly, the first principle must explain itself. It cannot be a principle which itself still requires explanation by something else. If it is itself not self-explanatory, but is an ultimate mystery, then even if we succeed in deducing the universe from it, nothing is thereby explained. This, for example, is precisely the defect of materialism. Even if we suppose it proved that all things, including mind, arise from matter, yet the objection remains that this explains nothing at all, for matter is not a self-explanatory existence. It is an unintelligible mystery. And to reduce the universe to an ultimate mystery is not to explain it. Again; some people think that the world is to be explained by what they call a "first cause." But why should any cause be the first? Why should we stop anywhere in the chain of causes? Every cause is necessarily the effect of a prior cause. The child, who is told that God made the world, and who inquires who, in that case, made God, is asking a highly sensible question. Or suppose, in tracing back the chain of causes, we come upon one which we have reason to say is really the first, is anything explained thereby? Still we are left with an ultimate mystery. Whatever the principle of explanation is, it cannot be a principle of this kind. It must be a principle which explains itself, and does not lead to something further, such as another cause. In other words, it must be a principle which has its whole being in itself, which does not for its completeness refer us to anything beyond itself. It must be something fully comprehended in itself, without reference to anything outside it. That is to say, it must be what we call self-determined or absolute. Now any absolute principle must necessarily be one. Suppose that it were two. Suppose you attempt to explain the world by two principles, X and Y, each of which is ultimate, neither being derived from the other. Then what relation does X bear to Y? We cannot fully comprehend X without knowing its relation to Y. Part of the character and being of X is constituted by its relation to Y. Part of X's character has to be explained by Y. But that is not to be self-explained. It is to be explained by something not itself. Therefore, the ultimate explanation of things must be one.

The Eleatics, then, were perfectly correct in saying that all is one, and that the ultimate principle of the universe, Being, is one. But if we examine the way in which they carried out their monism, we shall see that it broke down in a hopeless dualism. How did they explain the existence of the world? They propounded the principle of Being, as the ultimate reality. How then did they derive the actual world from that principle? The answer is that they neither derived it nor made any attempt to derive it. Instead of deducing the world from their first principle, they simply denied the reality of the world altogether. They attempted to solve the problem by denying the existence of the problem. The world, they said, is simply not-being. It is an illusion. Now certainly it is a great thing to know which is the true world, and which the false, but after all this is not an explanation. To call the world an illusion is not to explain it. If the world is reality, then the problem of philosophy is, how does that reality arise? If the world is illusion, then the problem is, how does that illusion arise? Call it illusion, if you like. But this is not explaining it. It is simply calling it names. This is the defect, too, of Indian philosophy in which the world is said to be Maya--delusion. Hence in the Eleatic philosophy there are two worlds brought face to face, lying side by side of each other, unreconciled--the world of Being, which is the true world, and the world of facts, which is illusion. Although the Eleatics deny the sense-world, and call it illusion, yet of this illusion they cannot rid themselves. In some sense or other, this world is here, is present. It comes back upon our senses, and demands explanation. Call it illusion, but it still stands beside the true world, and demands that it be deduced from that. So that the Eleatics have two principles, the false world and the true world, simply lying side by side, without any connecting link between them, without anything to show how the one arises from the other. It is an utterly irreconcilable dualism.

It is easy to see why the Eleatic philosophy broke down in this dualism. It is due to the barrenness of their first principle itself. Being, they say, has in it no becoming. All principle of motion is expressly excluded from it. Likewise they deny to it any multiplicity. It is simply one, without any many in it. If you expressly exclude multiplicity and becoming from your first principle, then you can never get multiplicity and becoming out of it. You cannot get out of it anything that is not in it. If you say absolutely there is no multiplicity in the Absolute, then it is impossible to explain how multiplicity comes into this world. It is exactly the same in regard to the question of quality. Pure Being is without quality. It is mere "isness." It is an utterly featureless, characterless Being, perfectly empty and abstract. How then can the quality of things issue from it? How can all the riches and variety of the world come out of this emptiness? The Eleatics are like jugglers who try to make you believe that they get rabbits, guinea-pigs, pieces of string, paper, and ribbon, out of an entirely empty top-hat. One can see how utterly barren and empty this principle is, if one translates it into figurative language, that is to say, into the language of religion. The Eleatic principle would correspond to a religion in which we said that "God is," but beyond the fact that He "is," He has absolutely no character. But surely this is a wholly barren and meagre conception of the Deity. In the Christian religion we are accustomed to hear such expressions as, not only that "God is," but that "God is Love," "God is Power," "God is Goodness," "God is Wisdom." Now objection may certainly be taken to these predicates and epithets on the ground that they are merely figurative and anthropomorphic. In fact, they exhibit the tendency to think non-sensuous objects sensuously. These predicates are merely picked up from the finite world and applied haphazard to God, for whom they are entirely inadequate. But at least these expressions teach us, that out of mere emptiness nothing can come; that the world cannot arise out of something which is lower and poorer than itself. Here in the world we find in a certain measure, love, wisdom, excellence, power. These things cannot spring from a source which is so poor that it contains nothing but "isness." The less can arise out of the greater, but not the greater out of the less. We may contrast Eleaticism not only with Christianity, but even with popular modern agnosticism. According to this, the Absolute is unknowable. But what the agnostic means is that human reason is inadequate to grasp the greatness of the ultimate being. But the Eleatic principle is, not that in saying "God is Love, Power, Wisdom," we are saying too little about God, and that our ideas are inadequate to express the fullness of His being, but on the contrary, that they express too high an idea for God, of whom nothing can be said except "He is," because there is absolutely nothing more to say. This conception of God is the conception of an absolutely empty being.

Monism, I said, is a necessary idea in philosophy. The Absolute must be one. But an utterly abstract monism is impossible. If the Absolute is simply one, wholly excludent of all process and multiplicity, out of such an abstraction the process and multiplicity of the world cannot issue. The Absolute is not simply one, or simply many. It must be a many in one, as correctly set forth in the Christian doctrine of the Trinity. Religion moves from an abstract polytheism (God is many) to an abstract monotheism (God is one; Judaism, Hinduism and Islam). But it does not stop there. It rightly passes on to a concrete monotheism (God is many in one; Christianity). There are two popular misconceptions regarding the doctrine of the Trinity. The first mistake is that of popular rationalism, the second is that of popular theology. Popular rationalism asserts that the doctrine of the Trinity is contrary to reason. Popular theology asserts that it is a mystery which transcends reason. But the truth is that it neither contradicts nor transcends reason. On the contrary, it is in itself the highest manifestation of reason. What is really a mystery, what really contradicts reason, is to suppose that God, the Absolute, is simply one without any multiplicity. This contradiction results in the fatal dualism which broke out in Eleaticism, and has broken out in every other system of thought, such as that of the Hindus or that of Spinoza, which begins with the conception of the Absolute as a pure one, totally exclusive of the many.

CHAPTER V

HERACLEITUS

Heracleitus was born about 535 B.C., and is believed to have lived to the age of sixty. This places his death at 475 B.C. He was thus subsequent to Xenophanes, contemporary with Parmenides, and older than Zeno. In historical order of time, therefore, he runs parallel to the Eleatics. Heracleitus was a man of Ephesus in Asia Minor. He was an aristocrat, descendant of a noble Ephesian family, and occupied in Ephesus the nominal position of basileus, or King. This, however, merely meant that he was the Chief Priest of the local branch of the Eleusinian mysteries, and this position he resigned in favour of his brother. He appears to have been a man of a somewhat aloof, solitary, and scornful nature. He looked down, not only upon the common herd, but even upon the great men of his own race. He mentions Xenophanes and Pythagoras in terms of obloquy. Homer, he thinks, should be taken out and whipped. Hesiod he considers to be the teacher of the common herd, one with them, "a man," he says, "who does not even know day and night." Upon the common herd of mortals he looks down with infinite scorn. Some of his sayings remind us not a little of Schopenhauer in their pungency and sharpness. "Asses prefer straw to gold." "Dogs bark at everyone they do not know." Many of his sayings, however, are memorable and trenchant epitomes of practical wisdom. "Man's character is his fate." "Physicians who cut, burn, stab and rack the sick, demand a fee for doing it, which they do not deserve to get." From his aloof and aristocratic standpoint he launched forth denunciations against the democracy of Ephesus.

Heracleitus embodied his philosophical thoughts in a prose treatise, which was well-known at the time of Socrates, but of which only fragments have come down to us. His style soon became proverbial for its difficulty and obscurity, and he gained the nickname of Heracleitus the "Dark," or the "Obscure." Socrates said of his work that what he understood of it was excellent, what not, he believed was equally so, but that the book required a tough swimmer. He has even been accused of intentional obscurity. But there does not seem to be any foundation for this charge. The fact is that if he takes no great trouble to explain his thoughts, neither does he take any trouble to conceal them. He does not write for fools. His attitude appears to be that if his readers understand him, well; if not, so much the worse for his readers. He wastes no time in elaborating and explaining his thought, but embodies it in short, terse, pithy, and pregnant sayings.

His philosophical principle is the direct antithesis of Eleaticism. The Eleatics had taught that only Being is, and Becoming is not at all. All change, all Becoming is mere illusion. For Heracleitus, on the contrary, only Becoming is, and Being, permanence, identity, these are nothing but illusion. All things sublunary are perpetually changing, passing over into new forms and new shapes. Nothing stands, nothing holds fast, nothing remains what it is. "Into the same river," he says, "we go down, and we do not go down; for into the same river no man can enter twice; ever it flows in and flows out." Not only does he deny all absolute permanence, but even a relative permanence of things is declared to be illusory. We all know that everything has its term, that all things arise and pass away, from the insects who live an hour to the "eternal" hills. Yet we commonly attribute to these things at least a relative permanence, a shorter or longer continuance in the same state. But even this Heracleitus will not allow. Nothing is ever the same, nothing remains identical from one consecutive moment to another. The appearance of relative permanence is an illusion, like that which makes us think that a wave passing over the surface of the water remains all the time the same identical wave. Here, as we know, the water of which the wave is composed changes from moment to moment, only the form remaining the same. Precisely so, for Heracleitus, the permanent appearance of things results from the inflow and outflow in them of equivalent quantities of substance. "All is flux." It is not, for example, the same sun which sets to-day and rises to-morrow. It is a new sun. For the fire of the sun burns itself out and is replenished from the vapours of the sea.

Not only do things change from moment to moment. Even in one and the same moment they are and are not the same. It is not merely that a thing first is, and then a moment afterwards, is not. It both is and is not at the same time. The at-onceness of "is" and "is not" is the meaning of Becoming. We shall understand this better if we contrast it with the Eleatic principle. The Eleatics described all things under two concepts, Being and not-being. Being has, for them, all truth, all reality. Not-being is wholly false and illusory. For Heracleitus both Being and not-being are equally real. The one is as true as the other. Both are true, for both are identical. Becoming is the identity of Being and not-being. For Becoming has only two forms, namely, the arising of things and their passing away, their beginning and their end, their origination and their decease. Perhaps you may think that this is not correct, that there are other forms of change besides origination and decease. A man is born. That is his origination. He dies. That is his decease. Between his birth and his death there are intermediate changes. He grows larger, grows older, grows wiser or more foolish, his hair turns grey. So also the leaf of a tree does not merely come into being and pass out of being. It changes in shape, form, colour. From light green it becomes dark green, and from dark green, yellow. But there is after all nothing in all this except origination and decease, not of the thing itself, but of its qualities. The change from green to yellow is the decease of green colour, the origination of yellow colour. Origination is the passage of not-being into Being. Decease is the passage of Being into not-being. Becoming, then, has in it only the two factors of Being and not-being, and it means the passing of one into the other. But this passage does not mean, for Heracleitus, that at one moment there is Being, and at the next moment not-being. It means that Being and not-being are in everything at one and the same time. Being is not-being. Being has not-being in it. Take as an example the problem of life and death. Ordinarily we think that death is due to external causes, such as accident or disease. We consider that while life lasts, it is what it is, and remains what it is, namely life, unmixed with death, and that it goes on being life until something comes from outside, as it were, in the shape of external causes, and puts an end to it. You may have read Metchnikoff's book "The Nature of Man." In the course of that book he develops this idea. Death, he says, is always due to external causes. Therefore, if we could remove the causes, we could conquer death. The causes of death are mostly disease and accident, for even old age is disease. There is no reason why science should not advance so far as to eliminate disease and accident from life. In that case life might be made immortal, or at any rate, indefinitely prolonged. Now this is founded upon a confusion of ideas. No doubt death is always due to external causes. Every event in the world is determined, and wholly determined, by causes. The law of causation admits of no exception whatever. Therefore it is perfectly true that in every case of death causes precede it. But, as I explained in the last chapter, to give the cause is not to give any reason for an event. Causation is never a principle of explanation of anything. It tells us that the phenomenon A is invariably and unconditionally followed by the phenomenon B, and we call A the cause of B. But this only means that whenever B happens, it happens in a certain regular order and succession of events. But it does not tell us why B happens at all. The reason of a thing is to be distinguished from its cause. The reason why a man dies is not to be found in the causes which bring about his death. The reason rather is that life has the germ of death already in it, that life is already death potentially, that Being has not-being in it. The causation of death is merely the mechanism, by the instrumentality of which, through one set of causes or another, the inevitable end is brought about.

Not only is Being, for Heracleitus, identical with not-being, but everything in the universe has in it its own opposite. Every existent thing is a "harmony of opposite tensions." A harmony contains necessarily two opposite principles which, in spite of their opposition, reveal an underlying unity. That it is by virtue of this principle that everything in the universe exists, is the teaching of Heracleitus. All things contain their own opposites within them. In the struggle and antagonism between hostile principles consists their life, their being, their very existence. At the heart of things is conflict. If there were no conflict in a thing, it would cease to exist. This idea is expressed by Heracleitus in a variety of ways. "Strife," he says, "is the father of all things." "The one, sundering from itself, coalesces with itself, like the harmony of the bow and the lyre." "God is day and night, summer and winter, war and peace, satiety and hunger." "Join together whole and unwhole, congruous and incongruous, accordant and discordant, then comes from one all and from all one." In this sense, too, he censures Homer for having prayed that strife might cease from among gods and men. If such a prayer were granted, the universe itself would pass away.

Side by side with this metaphysic, Heracleitus lays down a theory of physics. All things are composed of fire. "This world," he says, "neither one of the gods nor of the human race has made; but it is, it was, and ever shall be, an eternally living fire." All comes from fire, and to fire all returns. "All things are exchanged for fire and fire for all, as wares for gold and gold for wares." Thus there is only one ultimate kind of matter, fire, and all other forms of matter are merely modifications and variations of fire. It is clear for what reason Heracleitus enunciated this principle. It is an exact physical parallel to the metaphysical principle of Becoming. Fire is the most mutable of the elements. It does not remain the same from one moment to another. It is continually taking up matter in the form of fuel, and giving off equivalent matter in the form of smoke and vapour. The primal fire, according to Heracleitus, transmutes itself into air, air into water, and water into earth. This he calls "the downward path." To it corresponds "the upward path," the transmutation of earth into water, water to air, and air to fire. All transformation takes place in this regular order, and therefore, says Heracleitus, "the upward and the downward path are one."

Fire is further specially identified with life and reason. It is the rational element in things. The more fire there is, the more life, the more movement. The more dark and heavy materials there are, the more death, cold, and not-being. The soul, accordingly, is fire, and like all other fires it continually burns itself out and needs replenishment. This it obtains, through the senses and the breath, from the common life and reason of the world, that is, from the surrounding and all-pervading fire. In this we live and move and have our being. No man has a separate soul of his own. It is merely part of the one universal soul-fire. Hence if communication with this is cut off, man becomes irrational and finally dies. Sleep is the half-way house to death. In sleep the passages of the senses are stopped up, and the outer fire reaches us only through breath. Hence in sleep we become irrational and senseless, turning aside from the common life of the world, each to a private world of his own. Heracleitus taught also the doctrine of periodic world-cycles. The world forms itself out of fire, and by conflagration passes back to the primitive fire.

In his religious opinions Heracleitus was sceptical. But he does not, like Xenophanes, direct his attacks against the central ideas of religion, and the doctrine of the gods. He attacks mostly the outward observances and forms in which the religious spirit manifests itself. He inveighs against the worship of images, and urges the uselessness of blood sacrifice.

With the Eleatics he distinguishes between sense and reason, and places truth in rational cognition. The illusion of permanence he ascribes to the senses. It is by reason that we rise to the knowledge of the law of Becoming. In the comprehension of this law lies the duty of man, and the only road to happiness. Understanding this, man becomes resigned and contented. He sees that evil is the necessary counterpart of good, and pain the necessary counterpart of pleasure, and that both together are necessary to form the harmony of the world. Good and evil are principles on the struggle between which the very existence of things depends. Evil, too, is necessary, has its place in the world. To see this is to put oneself above pitiful and futile struggles against the supreme law of the universe.

CHAPTER VI
EMPEDOCLES

Empedocles was a man of Agrigentum in Sicily. The dates of his birth and death are placed about 495 and 435 B.C. respectively. Like Pythagoras, he possessed a powerful and magnetic personality. Hence all kinds of legends quickly grew up and wove themselves round his life and death. He was credited with the performance of miracles, and romantic stories were circulated about his death. A man of much persuasive eloquence he raised himself to the leadership of the Agrigentine democracy, until he was driven out into exile.

The philosophy of Empedocles is eclectic in character. Greek philosophy had now developed a variety of conflicting principles, and the task of Empedocles is to reconcile these, and to weld them together in a new system, containing however no new thought of its own. In speaking of Parmenides, I pointed out that his teaching may be interpreted either in an idealistic or a materialistic sense, and that these two aspects of thought lie side by side in Parmenides, and that it is possible to emphasize either the one or the other. Empedocles seizes upon the materialistic side. The essential thought of Parmenides was that Being cannot pass into not-being, nor not-being into Being. Whatever is, remains for ever what it is. If we take that in a purely material context, what it means is that matter has neither beginning nor end, is uncreated and indestructible. And this is the first basic principle of Empedocles. On the other hand, Heracleitus had shown that becoming and change cannot be denied. This is the second basic principle of Empedocles. That there is no absolute becoming, no creation, and utter destruction of things, and yet that things do somehow arise and pass away, this must be explained, these contradictory ideas must be reconciled. Now if we assert that matter is uncreated and indestructible, and yet that things arise and pass away, there is only one way of explaining this. We must suppose that objects, as wholes begin and cease to be, but that the material particles of which they are composed are uncreated and indestructible. This thought now forms the first principle of Empedocles, and of his successors, Anaxagoras, and the Atomists.

Now the Ionic philosophers had taught that all things are composed of some one ultimate matter. Thales believed it to be water, Anaximenes air. This necessarily involved that the ultimate kind of matter must be capable of transformation into other kinds of matter. If it is water, then water must be capable of turning into brass, wood, iron, air, or whatever other kind of matter exists. And the same thing applies to the air of Anaximenes. Parmenides, however, had taught that whatever is, remains always the same, no change or transformation being possible. Empedocles here too follows Parmenides, and interprets his doctrine in his own way. One kind of matter, he thinks, can never change into another kind of matter; fire never becomes water, nor does earth ever become air. This leads Empedocles at once to a doctrine of elements. The word "elements," indeed, is of later invention, and Empedocles speaks of the elements as "the roots of all." There are four elements, earth, air, fire, and water. Empedocles was therefore the originator of the familiar classification of the four elements. All other kinds of matter are to be explained as mixtures, in various proportions, of these four. Thus all origination and decease, as well as the differential qualities of certain kinds of matter, are now explained by the mixing and unmixing of the four elements. All becoming is simply composition and decomposition.

But the coming together and separation of the elements involves the movement of particles, and to explain this there must exist some moving force. The Ionic philosophers had assumed that matter has the power or force required for movement immanent in itself. The air of Anaximenes, of its own inherent power, transforms itself into other kinds of matter. This doctrine Empedocles rejects. Matter is for him absolutely dead and lifeless, without any principle of motion in itself. There is, therefore, only one remaining possibility. Forces acting upon matter from the outside must be assumed. And as the two essential processes of the world, mixing and unmixing, are opposite in character, so there must be two opposite forces. These he calls by the names Love and Hate, or Harmony and Discord. Though these terms may have an idealistic sound, Empedocles conceives them as entirely physical and material forces. But he identifies the attractions and repulsions of human beings, which we call love and hate, with the universally operating forces of the material world. Human love and hate are but the manifestations in us of the mechanical forces of attraction and repulsion at work in the world at large.

Empedocles taught the doctrine of periodic world-cycles. The world-process is, therefore, properly speaking, circular, and has neither beginning nor end. But in describing this process one must begin somewhere. We will begin, then, with the sphairos (sphere). In the primeval sphere the four elements are completely mixed, and interpenetrate each other completely. Water is not separated off from air, nor air from earth. All are chaotically mixed together. In any portion of the sphere there must be an equal quantity of earth, air, fire and water. The elements are thus in union, and the sole force operative within the sphere is Love or Harmony. Hence the sphere is called a "blessed god." Hate, however, exists all round the outside of the sphere. Hate gradually penetrates from the circumference towards the centre and introduces the process of separation and disunion of the elements. This process continues till, like coming together with like, the elements are wholly separated. All the water is together; all the fire is together, and so on. When this process of disintegration is complete, Hate is supreme and Love is entirely driven out. But Love again begins to penetrate matter, to cause union and mixture of the elements, and finally brings the world back to the state of the original sphere. Then the same process begins again. At what position in this circular movement is our present world to be placed? The answer is that it is neither in the complete union of the sphere, nor is it completely disintegrated. It is half-way between the sphere and the stage of total disintegration. It is proceeding from the former towards the later, and Hate is gradually gaining the upper hand. In the formation of the present world from the sphere the first element to be separated off was air, next fire, then the earth. Water is squeezed out of the earth by the rapidity of its rotation. The sky is composed of two halves. One is of fire, and this is the day. The other is dark matter with masses of fire scattered about in it, and this is the night.

Empedocles believed in the transmigration of souls. He also put forward a theory of sense-perception, the essential of which is that like perceives like.

The fire in us perceives external fire, and so with the other elements. Sight is caused by effluences of the fire and water of the eyes meeting similar effluences from external objects.

CHAPTER VII
THE ATOMISTS

The founder of the Atomist philosophy was Leucippus. Practically nothing is known of his life. The date of his birth, the date of his death, and his place of residence, are alike unknown, but it is believed that he was a contemporary of Empedocles and Anaxagoras. Democritus was a citizen of Abdera in Thrace. He was a man of the widest learning, as learning was understood in his day. A passion for knowledge and the possession of adequate means for the purpose, determined him to undertake extensive travels in order to acquire the wisdom and knowledge of other nations. He travelled largely in Egypt, also probably in Babylonia. The date of his death is unknown, but he certainly lived to a great age, estimated at from ninety to one hundred years. Exactly what were the respective contributions of Leucippus and Democritus to the Atomist philosophy, is also a matter of doubt. But it is believed that all the essentials of this philosophy were the work of Leucippus, and that Democritus applied and extended them, worked out details, and made the theory famous.

Now we saw that the philosophy of Empedocles was based upon an attempt to reconcile the doctrine of Parmenides with the doctrine of Heracleitus. The fundamental thought of Empedocles was that there is no absolute becoming in the strict sense, no passage of Being into not-being or not-being into Being. Yet the objects of the senses do, in some way, arise and pass away, and the only method by which this is capable of explanation is to suppose that objects, as whole objects, come to be and cease to be, but that the material particles of which they are composed are eternally existent. But the detailed development which Empedocles gave to this principle was by no means satisfactory. In the first place, if we hold that all objects are composed of parts, and that all becoming is due to the mixing and unmixing of pre-existent matter, we must have a theory of particles. And we do hear vaguely of physical particles in the doctrine of Empedocles, but no definition is given of their nature, and no clear conception is formed of their character. Secondly, the moving forces of Empedocles, Love and Hate, are fanciful and mythological. Lastly, though there are in Empedocles traces of the doctrine that the qualities of things depend on the position and arrangement of their particles, this idea is not consistently developed. For Empedocles there are only four ultimate kinds of matter, qualitatively distinguished. The differential qualities of all other kinds of matter must, therefore, be due to the mixing of these four elements. Thus the qualities of the four elements are ultimate and underived, but all other qualities must be founded upon the position and arrangement of particles of the four elements. This is the beginning of the mechanical explanation of quality. But to develop this theory fully and consistently, it should be shown, not merely that some qualities are ultimate and some derived from position and arrangement of particles, but that all quality whatever is founded upon position and arrangement. All becoming is explained by Empedocles as the result of motion of material particles. To bring this mechanical philosophy to its logical conclusion, all qualitativeness of things must be explained in the same way. Hence it was impossible that the philosophy of mechanism and materialism should stand still in the position in which Empedocles left it. It had to advance to the position of Atomism. The Atomists, therefore, maintain the essential position of Empedocles, after eliminating the inconsistencies which we have just noted. The philosophy of Empedocles is therefore to be considered as merely transitional in character.

First, the Atomists developed the theory of particles. According to Leucippus and Democritus, if matter were divided far enough, we should ultimately come to indivisible units. These indivisible units are called atoms, and atoms are therefore the ultimate constituents of matter. They are infinite in number, and are too small to be perceptible to the senses. Empedocles had assumed four different kinds of matter. But, for the Atomists, there is only one kind. All the atoms are composed of exactly the same kind of matter. With certain exceptions, which I will mention in a moment, they possess no quality. They are entirely non-qualitative, the only differences between them being differences of quantity. They differ in size, some being larger, some smaller. And they likewise differ in shape. Since the ultimate particles of things thus possess no quality, all the actual qualities of objects must be due to the arrangement and position of the atoms. This is the logical development of the tentative mechanism of Empedocles.

I said that the atoms possess no qualities. They must, however, be admitted to possess the quality of solidity, or impenetrability, since they are defined as being indivisible. Moreover it is a question whether the atoms of Democritus and Leucippus were thought to possess weight, or whether the weight of objects is to be explained, like other qualities, by the position and movement of the atoms. There is no doubt that the Epicureans of a later date considered the atoms to have weight. The Epicureans took over the atomism of Democritus and Leucippus, with few modifications, and made it the basis of their own teaching. They ascribed weight to the atoms, and the only question is whether this was a modification introduced by them, or whether it was part of the original doctrine of Democritus and Leucippus.

The atoms are bounded, and separated off from each other. Therefore, they must be separated by something, and this something can only be empty space. Moreover, since all becoming and all qualitativeness of things are to be explained by the mixing and unmixing of atoms, and since this involves movement of the atoms, for this reason also empty space must be assumed to exist, for nothing can move unless it has empty space to move in. Hence there are two ultimate realities, atoms and empty space. These correspond respectively to the Being and not-being of the Eleatics. But whereas the latter denied any reality to not-being, the Atomists affirm that not-being, that is, empty space, is just as real as being. Not-being also exists. "Being," said Democritus, "is by nothing more real than nothing." The atoms being non-qualitative, they differ in no respect from empty space, except that they are "full." Hence atoms and the void are also called the plenum and the vacuum.

How, now, is the movement of the atoms brought about? Since all becoming is due to the separation and aggregation of atoms, a moving force is required. What is this moving force? This depends upon the question whether atoms have weight. If we assume that they have weight, then the origin of the world, and the motion of atoms, becomes clear. In the system of the Epicureans the original movement of the atoms is due to their weight, which causes them to fall perpetually downwards through infinite space. Of course the Atomists had no true ideas of gravitation, nor did they understand that there is no absolute up and down. The large atoms are heavier than the smaller. The matter of which they are composed is always the same. Therefore, volume for volume, they weigh the same. Their weight is thus proportional to their size, and if one atom is twice as large as another, it will also be twice as heavy. Here the Atomists made another mistake, in supposing that heavier things fall in a vacuum more quickly than light things. They fall, as a matter of fact, with the same speed. But according to the Atomists, the heavier atoms, falling faster, strike against the lighter, and push them to one side and upwards. Through this general concussion of atoms a vortex is formed, in which like atoms come together with like. From the aggregation of atoms worlds are created. As space is infinite and the atoms go on falling eternally, there must have been innumerable worlds of which our world is only one. When the aggregated atoms fall apart again, this particular world will cease to exist. But all this depends upon the theory that the atoms have weight. According to Professor Burnet, however, the weight of atoms is a later addition of the Epicureans. If that is so, it is very difficult to say how the early Atomists, Leucippus and Democritus, explained the original motion. What was their moving force, if it was not weight? If the atoms have no weight, their original movement cannot have been a fall. "It is safest to say," says Professor Burnet, "that it is simply a confused motion this way and that." Probably this is a very safe thing to say, because it means nothing in particular. Motion itself cannot be confused. It is only our ideas of motion which can be confused. If this theory is correct, then, we can only say that the Atomists had no definite solution of the problem of the origin of motion and the character of the moving force. They apparently saw no necessity for explanation, which seems unlikely in view of the fact that Empedocles had already seen the necessity of solving the problem, and given a definite, if unsatisfactory, solution, in his theory of Love and Hate. This remark would apply to Democritus, if not to Leucippus.

The Atomists also spoke of all movement being under the force of "necessity." Anaxagoras was at this time teaching that all motion of things is produced by a world-intelligence, or reason. Democritus expressly opposes to this the doctrine of necessity. There is no reason or intelligence in the world. On the contrary, all phenomena and all becoming are completely determined by blind mechanical causes. In this connection there arises among the Atomists a polemic against the popular gods and the popular religion. Belief in gods Democritus explains as being due to fear of great terrestrial and astronomical phenomena, such as volcanoes, earthquakes, comets, and meteors. But somewhat inconsistently with this, Democritus believed that the air is inhabited by beings resembling men, but larger and of longer life, and explained belief in the gods as being due to projection from these of images of themselves composed of atoms which impinge upon human senses, and produce the ideas of gods.

Different kinds of matter must be explained, in any atomic theory, by the shape, size, and position of the atoms of which they are composed. Thus the Atomists taught that fire is composed of smooth round atoms. The soul is also composed of smooth round atoms, and is an exceptionally pure and refined fire. At death the soul atoms are scattered, and hence there is, of course, no question of a future life. Democritus also put forward a theory of perception, according to which objects project into space images of themselves composed of atoms. These images strike against the senses. Like atoms are perceived by like. Thought is true when the soul is equable in temperature. The sensible qualities of things, such as smell, taste, colour, do not exist in the things themselves, but merely express the manner in which they affect our senses, and are therefore relative to us. A number of the ethical maxims of Democritus have come down to us. But they are not based in any way upon the Atomic theory, and cannot be deduced from it. Hence they have no scientific foundation but are merely detached sayings, epitomizing the experience and worldly wisdom of Democritus. That one should enjoy oneself as much and vex oneself as little as possible seems to have been his principal idea. This, however, is not to be interpreted in any low, degraded, or sensual way. On the contrary, Democritus says that the happiness of man does not depend on material possessions, but upon the state of the soul. He praises equanimity and cheerfulness, and these are best attained, he thinks, by moderation and simplicity.

CHAPTER VIII
ANAXAGORAS

Anaxagoras was born at Clazomenae in Asia Minor about 500 B.C. He was a man of noble family, and possessed considerable property. He neglected his property in the search for knowledge and in the pursuit of science and philosophy. Leaving his home at Clazomenae, he settled down in Athens. We have not heard so far anything of Athens in the history of Greek Philosophy. It was Anaxagoras who transplanted philosophy to Athens, which from his time forward became the chief centre of Greek thought. At Athens, Anaxagoras came into contact with all the famous men of the time. He was an intimate friend of Pericles, the statesman, and of Euripides, the poet. But his friendship with Pericles cost him dear. There was a strong political faction opposed to Pericles. So far as we know Anaxagoras never meddled in politics, but he was a friend of the statesman Pericles, and that was quite enough. The enemies of Pericles determined to teach Anaxagoras a lesson, and a charge of atheism and blasphemy was accordingly brought against him. The particulars of the charge were that Anaxagoras said that the sun was a red-hot stone, and that the moon was made of earth. This was quite true, as that is exactly what Anaxagoras did say of the sun and the moon. But the Greeks regarded the heavenly bodies as gods; even Plato and Aristotle thought that the stars were divine beings. To call the sun a red-hot stone, and to say that the moon was made of earth, was therefore blasphemy according to Greek ideas. Anaxagoras was charged, tried, and condemned. The details of the trial, and of what followed, are not known with accuracy. But it appears that Anaxagoras escaped, probably with the help of Pericles, and from Athens went back to his native country in Asia Minor. He settled at Lampsacus, and died there at the age of 72. He was the author of a treatise in which he wrote down his philosophical ideas. This treatise was well-known at the time of Socrates, but only fragments now remain.

The foundation of the philosophy of Anaxagoras is the same as that of Empedocles and the Atomists. He denied any absolute becoming in the strict sense of the passing of being into not-being and not-being into being.

Matter is uncreated and indestructible, and all becoming must be accounted for by the mixing and unmixing of its component parts. This principle Anaxagoras himself expressed with great clearness, in a fragment of his treatise which has come down to us. "The Greeks," he says, "erroneously assume origination and destruction, for nothing originates and nothing is destroyed. All is only mixed and unmixed out of pre-existent things, and it were more correct to call the one process composition and the other process decomposition."

The Atomists had assumed the ultimate constituents of things to be atoms composed of the same kind of matter. Empedocles had believed in four ultimate and underived kinds of matter. With neither of these does Anaxagoras agree. For him, all the different kinds of matter are equally ultimate and underived, that is to say, such things as gold, bone, hair, earth, water, wood, etc., are ultimate kinds of matter, which do not arise from anything else, and do not pass over into one another. He also disagrees with the conception of the Atomists that if matter is divided far enough, ultimate and indivisible particles will be reached. According to Anaxagoras matter is infinitely divisible. In the beginning all these kinds of matter were mixed together in a chaotic mass. The mass stretches infinitely throughout space. The different kinds of matter wholly intermingle and interpenetrate each other. The process of world-formation is brought about by the unmixing of the conglomeration of all kinds of matter, and the bringing together of like matter with like. Thus the gold particles separating out of the mass come together, and form gold; the wood particles come together and form wood, and so on. But as matter is infinitely divisible and the original mixing of the elements was complete, they were, so to speak, mixed to an infinite extent. Therefore the process of unmixing would take infinite time, is now going on, and will always go on. Even in the purest element there is still a certain admixture of particles of other kinds of matter. There is no such thing as pure gold. Gold is merely matter in which the gold particles predominate.

As with Empedocles and the Atomists, a moving force is required to explain the world-process of unmixing. What, in the philosophy of

Anaxagoras, is this force? Now up to the present point the philosophy of Anaxagoras does not rise above the previous philosophies of Empedocles and the Atomists. On the contrary, in clearness and logical consistency, it falls considerably below the teaching of the latter. But it is just here, on the question of the moving force, that Anaxagoras becomes for the first time wholly original, and introduces a principle peculiar to himself, a principle, moreover, which is entirely new in philosophy. Empedocles had taken as his moving forces, Love and Hate, mythical and fanciful on the one hand, and yet purely physical on the other. The forces of the Atomists were also completely material. But Anaxagoras conceives the moving force as wholly non-physical and incorporeal. It is called Nous, that is, mind or intelligence. It is intelligence which produces the movement in things which brings about the formation of the world. What was it, now, which led Anaxagoras to the doctrine of a world-governing intelligence? It seems that he was struck with the apparent design, order, beauty and harmony of the universe. These things, he thought, could not be accounted for by blind forces. The world is apparently a rationally governed world. It moves towards definite ends. Nature shows plentiful examples of the adaptation of means to ends. There appears to be plan and purpose in the world. The Atomists had assumed nothing but matter and physical force. How can design, order, harmony and beauty be brought about by blind forces acting upon chaotic matter? Blind forces acting upon a chaos would produce motion and change. But the change would be meaningless and purposeless. They could not produce a rationally ordered cosmos. One chaos would succeed another chaos ad infinitum. That alone which can produce law and order is intelligence. There must therefore be a world-controlling Nous.

What is the character of the Nous, according to Anaxagoras? Is it, in the first place, really conceived as purely non-material and incorporeal? Aristotle, who was in a position to know more of the matter than any modern scholar, clearly implies in his criticism that the Nous of Anaxagoras is an incorporeal principle, and he has been followed in this by the majority of the best modern writers, such as Zeller and Erdmann. But the opposite view has been maintained, by Grote, for example, and more recently by Professor Burnet, who thinks that Anaxagoras conceived the Nous as a material and physical force. As the matter is of fundamental importance, I will mention the chief arguments upon which Professor Burnet rests his case. In the first place Anaxagoras described the Nous as the "thinnest and purest of all things." He also said that it was "unmixed," that it had in it no mixture of anything besides itself. Professor Burnet argues that such words as "thin" and "unmixed" would be meaningless in connection with an incorporeal principle. Only material things can properly be described as thin, pure, and unmixed. Secondly, Professor Burnet thinks that it is quite certain that the Nous occupies space, for Anaxagoras speaks of greater and smaller portions of it. Greater and smaller are spatial relations. Hence the Nous occupies space, and that which occupies space is material. But surely these are very inconclusive arguments. In the first place as regards the use of the words "thin" and "unmixed." It is true that these terms express primarily physical qualities. But, as I pointed out in the first chapter, almost all words by which we seek to express incorporeal ideas have originally a physical signification. And if Anaxagoras is to be called a materialist because he described the Nous as thin, then we must also plead guilty to materialism if we say that the thought of Plato is "luminous," or that the mind of Aristotle is "clear." The fact is that all philosophy labours under the difficulty of having to express non-sensuous thought in language which has been evolved for the purpose of expressing sensuous ideas. There is no philosophy in the world, even up to the present day, in which expressions could not be found in plenty which are based upon the use of physical analogies to express entirely non-physical ideas. Then as regards the Nous occupying space, it is not true that greater and smaller are necessarily spatial relations. They are also qualitative relations of degree. I say that the mind of Plato is greater than the mind of Callias. Am I to be called a materialist? Am I to be supposed to mean that Plato's mind occupies more space than that of Callias? And it is certainly in this way that Anaxagoras uses the terms. "All Nous," he says, "is alike, both the greater and the smaller." He means thereby that the world-forming mind (the greater) is identical in character with the mind of man (the smaller). For Anaxagoras it is the one Nous which animates all living beings, men, animals, and even plants. These different orders of beings are animated by the same Nous but in different degrees, that of man being the greatest. But this does not mean that the Nous in man occupies more space than the Nous in a plant. But even if Anaxagoras did conceive the Nous as spatial, it does not follow that he regarded it as material. The doctrine of the non-spatiality of mind is a modern doctrine, never fully developed till the time of Descartes. And to say that Anaxagoras did not realize that mind is non-spatial is merely to say that he lived before the time of Descartes. No doubt it would follow from this that the incorporeality of mind is vaguely and indistinctly conceived by Anaxagoras, that the antithesis between matter and mind is not so sharply drawn by him as it is by us. But still the antithesis is conceived, and therefore it is correct to say that the Nous of Anaxagoras is an incorporeal principle. The whole point of this introduction of the Nous into the philosophy of Anaxagoras is because he could not explain the design and order of the universe on a purely physical basis.

The next characteristic of Nous is that it is to be thought of as essentially the ground of motion. It is because he cannot in any other way explain purposive motion that Anaxagoras introduces mind into his otherwise materialistic system. Mind plays the part of the moving force which explains the world-process of unmixing. As the ground of motion, the Nous is itself unmoved; for if there were any motion in it we should have to seek for the ground of this motion in something else outside it. That which is the cause of all motion, cannot itself be moved. Next, the Nous is absolutely pure and unmixed with anything else. It exists apart, by itself, wholly in itself, and for itself. In contrast to matter, it is uncompounded and simple. It is this which gives it omnipotence, complete power over everything, because there is no mixture of matter in it to limit it, to clog and hinder its activities. We moderns are inclined to ask the question whether the Nous is personal. Is it, for example, a personal being like the God of the Christians? This is a question which it is almost impossible to answer. Anaxagoras certainly never considered it. According to Zeller, the Greeks had an imperfect and undeveloped conception of personality. Even in Plato we find the same difficulty. The antithesis between God as a personal and as an impersonal being, is a wholly modern idea. No Greek ever discussed it.

To come now to the question of the activity of the Nous and its function in the philosophy of Anaxagoras, we must note that it is essentially a world-forming, and not a world-creating, intelligence. The Nous and matter exist side by side from eternity. It does not create matter, but only arranges it. "All things were together," says Anaxagoras, "infinitely numerous, infinitely little; then came the Nous and set them in order." In this Anaxagoras showed a sound logical sense. He based his idea of the existence of Nous upon the design which exhibits itself in the world. In modern times the existence of design in the world has been made the foundation of an argument for the existence of God, which is known as the teleological argument. The word teleology means the view of things as adapting means towards purposive ends. To see intelligent design in the universe is to view the universe teleologically. And the teleological argument for the existence of God asserts that, as there is evidence of purpose in nature, this must be due to an intelligent cause. But, as a matter of fact, taken by itself, teleology cannot possibly be made the basis of an argument for the existence of a world-creating intelligence, but only for the existence of a world-designing intelligence. If you find in the desert the ruins of ancient cities and temples, you are entitled to conclude therefrom, that there existed a mind which designed these cities and buildings, and which arranged matter in that purposive way, but you are not entitled to conclude that the mind which designed the cities also created the matter out of which they were made. Anaxagoras was, therefore, in that sense quite right. Teleology is not evidence of a world-creating mind, and if we are to prove that, we must have recourse to other lines of reasoning.

In the beginning, then, there was a chaotic mixture of different kinds of matter. The Nous produced a vortex at one point in the middle of this mass. This vortex spread itself outwards in the mass of matter, like rings caused by the fall of a stone in water. It goes on for ever and continually draws more and more matter out of the infinite mass into itself. The movement, therefore, is never-ending. It causes like kinds of matter to come together with like, gold to gold, wood to wood, water to water, and so on. It is to be noted, therefore, that the action of the Nous is apparently confined to the first movement. It acts only at the one central point, and every subsequent movement is caused by the vortex itself, which draws in more and more of the surrounding matter into itself. First are separated out the warm, dry, and light particles, and these form the aether or upper air. Next come the cold, moist, dark, and dense particles which form the lower air. Rotation takes the latter towards the centre, and out of this the earth is formed. The earth, as with Anaximenes, is a flat disc, borne upon the air. The heavenly bodies consist of masses of stone which have been torn from the earth by the force of its rotation, and being projected outwards become incandescent through the rapidity of their movement. The moon is made of earth and reflects the light of the sun. Anaxagoras was thus the first to give the true cause of the moon's light. He was also the first to discover the true theory of eclipses, since he taught that the solar eclipse is due to the intervention of the moon between the sun and the earth, and that lunar eclipses arise from the shadow of the earth falling upon the moon. He believed that there are other worlds besides our own with their own suns and moons. These worlds are inhabited. The sun, according to Anaxagoras, is many times as large as the Peloponnese. The origin of life upon the earth is accounted for by germs which existed in the atmosphere, and which were brought down into the terrestrial slime by rain water, and there fructified. Anaxagoras's theory of perception is the opposite of the theories of Empedocles and the Atomists. Perception takes place by unlike matter meeting unlike.

Anaxagoras owes his importance in the history of philosophy to the theory of the Nous. This was the first time that a definite distinction had been made between the corporeal and incorporeal. Anaxagoras is the last philosopher of the first period of Greek philosophy. In the second chapter, I observed that this first period is characterized by the fact that in it the Greek mind looks only outward upon the external world. It attempts to explain the operations of nature. It had not yet learned to look inward upon itself. But the transition to the introspective study of mind is found in the Nous of Anaxagoras. Mind is now brought to the fore as a problem for philosophy. To find reason, intelligence, mind, in all things, in the State, in the individual, in external nature, this is the characteristic of the second period of Greek philosophy. To have formulated the antithesis between mind and matter is the most important work of Anaxagoras.

Secondly, it is to the credit of Anaxagoras that he was the first to introduce the idea of teleology into philosophy. The system of the Atomists formed the logical completion of the mechanical theory of the world. The theory of mechanism seeks to explain all things by causes. But, as we saw, causation can explain nothing. The mechanism of the world shows us by what means events are brought about, but it does not explain why they are brought about at all. That can only be explained by showing the reason for things, by exhibiting all process as a means towards rational ends. To look to the beginning (cause) of things for their explanation is the theory of mechanism. To look to their ends for explanation of them is teleology. Anaxagoras was the first to have dimly seen this. And for this reason Aristotle praises him, and, contrasting him with the mechanists, Leucippus and Democritus, says that he appears like "a sober man among vain babblers." The new principle which he thus introduced into philosophy was developed, and formed the central idea of Plato and Aristotle. To have realized the twin antitheses of matter and mind, of mechanism and teleology, is the glory of Anaxagoras.

But it is just here, in the development of these two ideas, that the defects of his system make their appearance. Firstly, he so separated matter and mind that his philosophy ends in sheer dualism. He assumes the Nous and matter as existing from the beginning, side by side, as equally ultimate and underived principles. A monistic materialism would have derived the Nous from matter, and a monistic idealism would have derived matter from the Nous. But Anaxagoras does neither. Each is left, in his theory, an inexplicable ultimate mystery. His philosophy is, therefore, an irreconcilable dualism.

Secondly, his teleology turns out in the end to be only a new theory of mechanism. The only reason which induces him to introduce the Nous into the world, is because he cannot otherwise explain the origin of movement.

It is only the first movement of things, the formation of the vortex, which he explains by mind. All subsequent process is explained by the action of the vortex itself, which draws the surrounding matter into itself. The Nous is thus nothing but another piece of mechanism to account for the first impulse to motion. He regards the Nous simply as a first cause, and thus the characteristic of all mechanism, to look back to first causes, to the beginning, rather than to the end of things for their explanation, appears here. Aristotle, as usual, puts the matter in a nutshell. "Anaxagoras," he says, "uses mind as a deus ex machina to account for the formation of the world, and whenever he is at a loss to explain why anything necessarily is, he drags it in by force. But in other cases he assigns as a cause for things anything else in preference to mind."

CHAPTER IX
THE SOPHISTS

The first period of Greek philosophy closes with Anaxagoras. His doctrine of the world-forming intelligence introduced a new principle into philosophy, the principle of the antithesis between corporeal matter and incorporeal mind, and therefore, by implication, the antithesis between nature and man. And if the first period of philosophy has for its problem the origin of the world, and the explanation of the being and becoming of nature, the second period of philosophy opens, in the Sophists, with the problem of the position of man in the universe. The teaching of the earlier philosophers was exclusively cosmological, that of the Sophists exclusively humanistic. Later in this second period, these two modes of thought come together and fructify one another. The problem of the mind and the problem of nature are subordinated as factors of the great, universal, all-embracing, world-systems of Plato and Aristotle.

It is not possible to understand the activities and teaching of the Sophists without some knowledge of the religious, political, and social conditions of the time. After long struggles between the people and the nobles, democracy had almost everywhere triumphed. But in Greece democracy did not mean what we now mean by that word. It did not mean representative institutions, government by the people through their elected deputies. Ancient Greece was never a single nation under a single government. Every city, almost every hamlet, was an independent State, governed only by its own laws. Some of these States were so small that they comprised merely a handful of citizens. All were so small that all the citizens could meet together in one place, and themselves in person enact the laws and transact public business. There was no necessity for representation. Consequently in Greece every citizen was himself a politician and a legislator. In these circumstances, partisan feeling ran to extravagant lengths. Men forgot the interests of the State in the interests of party, and this ended in men forgetting the interests of their party in their own interests. Greed, ambition, grabbing, selfishness, unrestricted egotism, unbridled avarice, became the dominant notes of the political life of the time.

Hand in hand with the rise of democracy went the decay of religion. Belief in the gods was almost everywhere discredited. This was partly due to the moral worthlessness of the Greek religion itself. Any action, however scandalous or disgraceful, could be justified by the examples of the gods themselves as related by the poets and mythologers of Greece. But, in greater measure, the collapse of religion was due to that advance of science and philosophy which we have been considering in these lectures. The universal tendency of that philosophy was to find natural causes for what had hitherto been ascribed to the action of the divine powers, and this could not but have an undermining effect upon popular belief. Nearly all the philosophers had been secretly, and many of them openly, antagonistic to the people's religion. The attack was begun by Xenophanes; Heracleitus carried it on; and lastly Democritus had attempted to explain belief in the gods as being caused by fear of gigantic terrestrial and astronomical phenomena. No educated man any longer believed in divination, auguries, and miracles. A wave of rationalism and scepticism passed over the Greek people. The age became one of negative, critical, and destructive thought. Democracy had undermined the old aristocratic institutions of the State, and science had undermined religious orthodoxy. With the downfall of these two pillars of things established, all else went too. All morality, all custom, all authority, all tradition, were criticised and rejected. What was regarded with awe and pious veneration by their fore-fathers the modern Greeks now looked upon as fit subjects for jest and mockery. Every restraint of custom, law, or morality, was resented as an unwarrantable restriction upon the natural impulses of man. What alone remained when these were thrust aside were the lust, avarice, and self-will of the individual.

The teaching of the Sophists was merely a translation into theoretical propositions of these practical tendencies of the period. The Sophists were the children of their time, and the interpreters of their age. Their philosophical teachings were simply the crystallization of the impulses which governed the life of the people into abstract principles and maxims.

Who and what were the Sophists? In the first place, they were not a school of philosophers. They are not to be compared, for example, with the Pythagoreans or Eleatics. They had not, as a school has, any system of philosophy held in common by them all. None of them constructed systems of thought. They had in common only certain loose tendencies of thought. Nor were they, as we understand the members of a school to be, in any close personal association with one another. They were a professional class rather than a school, and as such they were scattered over Greece, and nourished among themselves the usual professional rivalries. They were professional teachers and educators. The rise of the Sophists was due to the growing demand for popular education, which was partly a genuine demand for light and knowledge, but was mostly a desire for such spurious learning as would lead to worldly, and especially political, success. The triumph of democracy had brought it about that political careers were now open to the masses who had hitherto been wholly shut out from them. Any man could rise to the highest positions in the State, if he were endowed with cleverness, ready speech, whereby to sway the passions of the mob, and a sufficient equipment in the way of education. Hence the demand arose for such an education as would enable the ordinary man to carve out a political career for himself. It was this demand which the Sophists undertook to satisfy. They wandered about Greece from place to place, they gave lectures, they took pupils, they entered into disputations. For these services they exacted large fees. They were the first in Greece to take fees for the teaching of wisdom. There was nothing disgraceful in this in itself, but it had never been customary. The wise men of Greece had never accepted any payment for their wisdom. Socrates, who never accepted any payment, but gave his wisdom freely to all who sought it, somewhat proudly contrasted himself with the Sophists in this respect.

The Sophists were not, technically speaking, philosophers. They did not specialise in the problems of philosophy. Their tendencies were purely practical. They taught any subject whatever for the teaching of which there was a popular demand. For example, Protagoras undertook to impart to his pupils the principles of success as a politician or as a private citizen. Gorgias taught rhetoric and politics, Prodicus grammar and etymology, Hippias history, mathematics and physics. In consequence of this practical tendency of the Sophists we hear of no attempts among them to solve the problem of the origin of nature, or the character of the ultimate reality. The Sophists have been described as teachers of virtue, and the description is correct, provided that the word virtue is understood in its Greek sense, which did not restrict it to morality alone. For the Greeks, it meant the capacity of a person successfully to perform his functions in the State. Thus the virtue of a mechanic is to understand machinery, the virtue of a physician to cure the sick, the virtue of a horse trainer the ability to train horses. The Sophists undertook to train men to virtue in this sense, to make them successful citizens and members of the State.

But the most popular career for a Greek of ability at the time was the political, which offered the attraction of high positions in the State. And for this career what was above all necessary was eloquence, or if that were unattainable, at least ready speech, the ability to argue, to meet every point as it arose, if not with sound reasoning, then with quick repartee. Hence the Sophists very largely concentrated their energies upon the teaching of rhetoric. In itself this was good. They were the first to direct attention to the science of rhetoric, of which they may be considered the founders. But their rhetoric also had its bad side, which indeed, soon became its only side. The aims of the young politicians whom they trained were, not to seek out the truth for its own sake, but merely to persuade the multitude of whatever they wished them to believe. Consequently the Sophists, like lawyers, not caring for the truth of the matter, undertook to provide a stock of arguments on any subject, or to prove any proposition. They boasted of their ability to make the worse appear the better reason, to prove that black is white. Some of them, like Gorgias, asserted that it was not necessary to have any knowledge of a subject to give satisfactory replies as regards it. And Gorgias ostentatiously undertook to answer any question on any subject instantly and without consideration. To attain these ends mere quibbling, and the scoring of verbal points, were employed. Hence our word "sophistry." The Sophists, in this way, endeavoured to entangle, entrap, and confuse their opponents, and even, if this were not possible, to beat them down by mere violence and noise. They sought also to dazzle by means of strange or flowery metaphors, by unusual figures of speech, by epigrams and paradoxes, and in general by being clever and smart, rather than earnest and truthful. When a man is young he is often dazzled by brilliance and cleverness, by paradox and epigram, but as he grows older he learns to discount these things and to care chiefly for the substance and truth of what is said. And the Greeks were a young people. They loved clever sayings. And this it is which accounts for the toleration which they extended even to the most patent absurdities of the Sophists. The modern question whether a man has ceased beating his wife is not more childish than many of the rhetorical devices of the Sophists, and is indeed characteristic of the methods of the more extravagant among them.

The earliest known Sophist is Protagoras. He was born at Abdera, about 480 B.C. He wandered up and down Greece, and settled for some time at Athens. At Athens, however, he was charged with impiety and atheism. This was on account of a book written by him on the subject of the gods, which began with the words, "As for the gods, I am unable to say whether they exist or whether they do not exist." The book was publicly burnt, and Protagoras had to fly from Athens. He fled to Sicily, but was drowned on the way about the year 410 B.C.

Protagoras was the author of the famous saying, "Man is the measure of all things; of what is, that it is; of what is not, that it is not." Now this saying puts in a nutshell, so to speak, the whole teaching of Protagoras. And, indeed, it contains in germ the entire thought of the Sophists. It is well, therefore, that we should fully understand exactly what it means. The earlier Greek philosophers had made a clear distinction between sense and thought, between perception and reason, and had believed that the truth is to be found, not by the senses, but by reason. The Eleatics had been the first to emphasize this distinction. The ultimate reality of things, they said, is pure Being, which is known only through reason; it is the senses which delude us with a show of becoming. Heracleitus had likewise affirmed that the truth, which was, for him, the law of becoming, is known by thought, and that it is the senses which delude us with a show of permanence. Even Democritus believed that true being, that is, material atoms, are so small that the senses cannot perceive them, and only reason is aware of their existence. Now the teaching of Protagoras really rests fundamentally upon the denying and confusing of this distinction. If we are to see this, we must first of all understand that reason is the universal, sensation the particular, element in man. In the first place, reason is communicable, sensation incommunicable. My sensations and feelings are personal to myself, and cannot be imparted to other people. For example, no one can communicate the sensation of redness to a colour-blind man, who has not already experienced it. But a thought, or rational idea, can be communicated to any rational being. Now suppose the question is whether the angles at the base of an isosceles triangle are equal. We may approach the problem in two ways. We may appeal either to the senses or to reason. If we appeal to the senses, one man will come forward and say that to him the angles look equal. Another man will say that one angle looks bigger than the other, and so on. But if, like Euclid, we appeal to reason, then it can be proved that the two angles are equal, and there is no room left for mere personal impressions, because reason is a law universally valid and binding upon all men. My sensations are private and peculiar to myself. They bind no one but myself. My impressions about the triangle are not a law to anyone except myself. But my reason I share with all other rational beings. It is not a law for me merely, but for all. It is one and the same reason in me and in other men. Reason, therefore, is the universal, sensation the particular, element in man. Now it is practically this distinction that Protagoras denied. Man, he said, is the measure of all things. By man he did not mean mankind at large. He meant the individual man. And by measure of all things he meant the standard of the truth of all things. Each individual man is the standard of what is true to himself. There is no truth except the sensations and impressions of each man. What seems true to me is true for me. What seems true to you is true for you.

We commonly distinguish between subjective impressions and objective truth. The words subjective and objective are constantly recurring throughout the history of philosophy, and as this is the first time I use them, I will explain them here. In every act of thought there must necessarily be two terms. I am now looking at this desk and thinking of this desk. There is the "I" which thinks, and there is the desk which is thought. "I" am the subject of the thought, the desk is the object of the thought. In general, the subject is that which thinks, and the object is that which is thought. Subjective is that which appertains to the subject, and objective is that which appertains to the object. So the meaning of the distinction between subjective impressions and the objective truth is clear. My personal impression may be that the earth is flat, but the objective truth is that the earth is round. Travelling through a desert, I may be subject to a mirage, and think that there is water in front of me. That is my subjective impression. The objective truth is that there is nothing but sand. The objective truth is something which has an existence of its own, independent of me. It does not matter what I think, or what you think, what I want, or what you want; the truth is what it is. We must conform ourselves to the truth. Truth will not conform itself to our personal inclinations, wishes, or impressions. The teaching of Protagoras practically amounted to a denial of this. What it meant was that there is no objective truth, no truth independent of the individual subject. Whatever seems to the individual true is true for that individual. Thus truth is identified with subjective sensations and impressions.

To deny the distinction between objective truth and subjective impression is the same as to deny the distinction between reason and sense. To my senses the earth seems flat. It looks flat to the eye. It is only through reason that I know the objective truth that the world is round. Reason, therefore, is the only possible standard of objective truth. If you deny the rational element its proper part, it follows that you will be left a helpless prey to diverse personal impressions. The impressions yielded by the senses differ in different people. One man sees a thing in one way, another sees it in another. If, therefore, what seems to me true is true for me, and what seems to you true is true for you, and if our impressions differ, it will follow that two contradictory propositions must both be true. Protagoras clearly understood this, and did not flinch from the conclusion. He taught that all opinions are true, that error is impossible, and that, whatever proposition is put forward, it is always possible to oppose to it a contradictory proposition with equally good arguments and with equal truth. In reality, the result of this procedure is to rob the distinction between truth and falsehood of all meaning. It makes no difference whether we say that all opinions are true, or whether we say that all are false. The words truth and falsehood, in such context, have no meaning. To say that whatever I feel is the truth for me means only that what I feel I feel. To call this "truth for me," adds nothing to the meaning.

Protagoras seems to have been led to these doctrines partly by observing the different accounts of the same object which the sense-organs yield to different people, and even to the same person at different times. If knowledge depends upon these impressions, the truth about the object cannot be ascertained. He was also influenced by the teaching of Heracleitus. Heracleitus had taught that all permanence is illusion. Everything is a perpetual becoming; all things flow. What is at this moment, at the next moment is not. Even at one and the same moment, Heracleitus believed, a thing is and is not. If it is true to say that it is, it is equally true that it is not. And this is, in effect, the teaching of Protagoras.

The Protagorean philosophy thus amounts to a declaration that knowledge is impossible. If there is no objective truth, there cannot be any knowledge of it. The impossibility of knowledge is also the standpoint of Gorgias. The title of his book is characteristic of the Sophistical love of paradox. It was called "On Nature, or the non-existent." In this book he attempted to prove three propositions, (1) that nothing exists: (2) that if anything exists, it cannot be known: (3) that if it can be known, the knowledge of it cannot be communicated.

For proof of the first proposition, "nothing exists," Gorgias attached himself to the school of the Eleatics, especially to Zeno. Zeno had taught that in all multiplicity and motion, that is to say, in all existence, there are irreconcilable contradictions. Zeno was in no sense a sceptic. He did not seek for contradictions in things for the sake of the contradictions, but in order to support the positive thesis of Parmenides, that only being is, and that becoming is not at all. Zeno, therefore, is to be regarded as a constructive, and not merely as a destructive, thinker. But it is obvious that by emphasizing only the negative element in his philosophy, it is possible to use his antinomies as powerful weapons in the cause of scepticism and nihilism. And it was in this way that Gorgias made use of the dialectic of Zeno. Since all existence is self-contradictory, it follows that nothing exists. He also made use of the famous argument of Parmenides regarding the origin of being. If anything is, said Gorgias, it must have had a beginning. Its being must have arisen either from being, or from not-being. If it arose from being, there is no beginning. If it arose from not-being, this is impossible, since something cannot arise out of nothing. Therefore nothing exists.

The second proposition of Gorgias, that if anything exists it cannot be known, is part and parcel of the whole Sophistic tendency of thought, which identifies knowledge with sense-perception, and ignores the rational element. Since sense-impressions differ in different people, and even in the same person, the object as it is in itself cannot be known. The third proposition follows from the same identification of knowledge with sensation, since sensation is what cannot be communicated.

The later Sophists went much further than Protagoras and Gorgias. It was their work to apply the teaching of Protagoras to the spheres of politics and morals. If there is no objective truth, and if what seems true to each individual is for him the truth, so also, there can be no objective moral code, and what seems right to each man is right for him. If we are to have anything worth calling morality, it is clear that it must be a law for all, and not merely a law for some. It must be valid for, and binding upon, all men. It must, therefore, be founded upon that which is universal in man, that is to say, his reason. To found it upon sense-impressions and feelings is to found it upon shifting quicksands. My feelings and sensations are binding upon no man but myself, and therefore a universally valid law cannot be founded upon them. Yet the Sophists identified morality with the feelings of the individual. Whatever I think right is right for me. Whatever you think right is right for you. Whatever each man, in his irrational self-will, chooses to do, that is, for him, legitimate. These conclusions were drawn by Polus, Thrasymachus, and Critias.

Now if there is, in this way, no such thing as objective right, it follows that the laws of the State can be founded upon nothing except force, custom, and convention. We often speak of just laws, and good laws. But to speak in that way involves the existence of an objective standard of goodness and justice, with which we can compare the law, and see whether it agrees with that standard or not. To the Sophists, who denied any such standard, it was mere nonsense to speak of just and good laws. No law is in itself good or just, because there is no such thing as goodness or justice. Or if they used such a word as justice, they defined it as meaning the right of the stronger; or the right of the majority. Polus and Thrasymachus, consequently, drew the conclusion that the laws of the State were inventions of the weak, who were cunning enough, by means of this stratagem, to control the strong, and rob them of the natural fruits of their strength. The law of force is the only law which nature recognizes. If a man, therefore, is powerful enough to defy the law with impunity, he has a perfect right to do so. The Sophists were thus the first, but not the last, to preach the doctrine that might is right. And, in similar vein, Critias explained popular belief in the gods as the invention of some crafty statesman for controlling the mob through fear.

Now it is obvious that the whole tendency of this sophistical teaching is destructive and anti-social. It is destructive of religion, of morality, of the foundations of the State, and of all established institutions. And we can now see that the doctrines of the Sophists were, in fact, simply the crystallization into abstract thought of the practical tendencies of the age. The people in practice, the Sophists in theory, decried and trod under foot the restrictions of law, authority, and custom, leaving nothing but the deification of the individual in his crude self-will and egotism. It was in fact an age of "aufklärung," which means enlightenment or illumination. Such periods of illumination, it seems, recur periodically in the history of thought, and in the history of civilization. This is the first, but not the last, such period with which the history of philosophy deals. This is the Greek illumination. Such periods present certain characteristic features. They follow, as a rule, upon an era of constructive thought. In the present instance the Greek illumination followed closely upon the heels of the great development of science and philosophy from Thales to Anaxagoras. In such a constructive period the great thinkers bring to birth new principles, which, in the course of time, filter down to the masses of the people and cause popular, if shallow, science, and a wide-spread culture. Popular education becomes a feature of the time. The new ideas, fermenting among the people, break up old prejudices and established ideas, and thus thought, at first constructive, becomes, among the masses, destructive in character. Hence the popular thought, in a period of enlightenment, issues in denial, scepticism, and disbelief. It is merely negative in its activities and results. Authority, tradition, and custom are wholly or partially destroyed. And since authority, tradition, and custom are the cement of the social structure, there results a general dissolution of that structure into its component individuals. All emphasis is now laid on the individual. Thought becomes egocentric. Individualism is the dominant note. Extreme subjectivity is the principle of the age. All these features make their appearance in the Greek aufklärung. The Sophistical doctrine that the truth is what I think, the good what I choose to do, is the extreme application of the subjective and egocentric principles.

The early eighteenth century in England and France was likewise a period of enlightenment, and the era from which we are now, perhaps, just emerging, bears many of the characteristics of aufklärung. It is sceptical and destructive. All established institutions, marriage, the family, the state, the law, come in for much destructive criticism. It followed immediately upon the close of a great period of constructive thought, the scientific development of the nineteenth century. And lastly, the age has produced its own Protagorean philosophy, which it calls pragmatism. If pragmatism is not egocentric, it is at least anthropocentric. Truth is no longer thought of as an objective reality, to which mankind must conform. On the contrary, the truth must conform itself to mankind. Whatever it is useful to believe, whatever belief "works" in practice, is declared to be true. But since what "works" in one age and country does not "work" in another, since what it is useful to believe to-day will be useless to-morrow, it follows that there is no objective truth independent of mankind at all. Truth is not now defined as dependent on the sensations of man, as it was with Protagoras, but as dependent on the volition of man. In either case it is not the universal in man, his reason, which is made the basis of truth and morals, but the subjective, individual, particular element in him.

We must not forget the many merits of the Sophists. Individually, they were often estimable men. Nothing is known against the character of Protagoras, and Prodicus was proverbial for his wisdom and the genuine probity and uprightness of his principles. Moreover the Sophists contributed much to the advance of learning. They were the first to direct attention to the study of words, sentences, style, prosody, and rhythm. They were the founders of the science of rhetoric. They spread education and culture far and wide in Greece, they gave a great impulse to the study of ethical ideas, which made possible the teaching of Socrates, and they stirred up a ferment of ideas without which the great period of Plato and Aristotle could never have seen the light. But, from the philosophical point of view, their merit is for the first time to have brought into general recognition the right of the subject. For there is, after all, much reason in these attacks made by the Sophists upon authority, upon established things, upon tradition, custom and dogma. Man, as a rational being, ought not to be tyrannized over by authority, dogma, and tradition. He cannot be subjected, thus violently, to the imposition of beliefs from an external source. No man has the right to say to me, "you shall think this," or "you shall think that." I, as a rational being, have the right to use my reason, and judge for myself. If a man would convince me, he must not appeal to force, but to reason. In doing so, he is not imposing his opinions externally upon me; he is educing his opinions from the internal sources of my own thought; he is showing me that his opinions are in reality my own opinions, if I only knew it. But the mistake of the Sophists was that, in thus recognizing the right of the subject, they wholly ignored and forgot the right of the object. For the truth has objective existence, and is what it is, whether I think it or not. Their mistake was that though they rightly saw that for truth and morality to be valid for me, they must be assented to by, and developed out of, me myself, not imposed from the outside, yet they laid the emphasis on my merely accidental and particular characteristics, my impulses, feelings, and sensations, and made these the source of truth and morality, instead of emphasizing as the source of truth and right the universal part of me, my reason. "Man is the measure of all things"; certainly, but man as a rational being, not man as a bundle of particular sensations, subjective impressions, impulses, irrational prejudices, self-will, mere eccentricities, oddities, foibles, and fancies.

Good examples of the right and wrong principles of the Sophists are to be found in modern Protestantism and modern democracy. Protestantism, it is often said, is founded upon the right of private judgment, and this is simply the right of the subject, the right of the individual to exercise his own reason. But if this is interpreted to mean that each individual is entitled to set up his mere whims and fancies as the law in religious matters, then we have the bad sort of Protestantism. Again, democracy is simply political protestantism, and democratic ideas are the direct offspring of the protestant Reformation. The democratic principle is that no rational being can be asked to obey a law to which his own reason has not assented. But the law must be founded upon reason, upon the universal in man. I, as an individual, as a mere ego, have no rights whatever. It is only as a rational being, as a potentially universal being, as a member of the commonwealth of reason, that I have any rights, that I can claim to legislate for myself and others. But if each individual's capricious self-will, his mere whims and fancies, are erected into a law, then democracy turns into anarchism and bolshevism.

It is a great mistake to suppose that the doctrines of the Sophists are merely antiquated ideas, dead and fossilized thoughts, of interest only to historians, but of no importance to us. On the contrary, modern popular thought positively reeks with the ideas and tendencies of the Sophists. It is often said that a man ought to have strong convictions, and some people even go so far as to say that it does not much matter what a man believes, so long as what he believes he believes strongly and firmly. Now certainly it is quite true that a man with strong convictions is more interesting than a man without any opinions. The former is at least a force in the world, while the latter is colourless and ineffectual. But to put exclusive emphasis on the mere fact of having convictions is wrong. After all, the final test of worth must be whether the man's convictions are true or false. There must be an objective standard of truth, and to forget this, to talk of the mere fact of having strong opinions as in itself a merit, is to fall into the error of the Sophists.

Another common saying is that everyone has a right to his own opinions. This is quite true, and it merely expresses the right of the subject to use his own reason. But it is sometimes interpreted in a different way. If a man holds a totally irrational opinion, and if every weapon is beaten out of his hands, if he is driven from every position he takes up--so that there is nothing left for him to do, except to admit that he is wrong, such a man will sometimes take refuge in the saying, that, after all, argue as you may, he has a right to his own opinion. But we cannot allow the claim. No man has a right to wrong opinions. There cannot be any right in wrong opinions. You have no right to an opinion unless it is founded upon that which is universal in man, his reason. You cannot claim this right on behalf of your subjective impressions, and irrational whims. To do so is to make the mistake of the Sophists.

The tendencies of the more shallow type of modern rationalism exhibit a similar Sophistical thought. It is pointed out that moral ideas vary very much in different countries and ages, that in Japan, for example, prostitution is condoned, and that in ancient Egypt incest was not condemned. Now it is important to know these facts. They should serve as a warning to us against dogmatic narrow-mindedness in moral matters. But some people draw from these facts the conclusion that there is no universally valid and objectively real moral law. The conclusion does not follow from the premises, and the conclusion is false. People's opinions differ, not only on moral questions, but upon every subject under the sun. Because men, a few hundred years ago, believed that the earth was flat, whereas now we believe it is round, it does not follow that it has in reality no shape at all, that there is no objective truth in the matter. And because men's opinions differ, in different ages and countries, as to what the true moral law is, it does not follow that there is no objective moral law.

We will take as our last example the current talk about the importance of developing one's personality. A man, it is said, should "be himself," and the expression of his own individuality must be his leading idea. Now certainly it is good to be oneself in the sense that it is hypocritical to pretend to be what one is not. Moreover, it is no doubt true that each man has certain special gifts, which he ought to develop, so that all, in their diverse ways, may contribute as much as possible to the spiritual and material wealth of the world. But this ideal of individuality often leads to false developments, as we see in the spheres of art and of education. Such a man as Oscar Wilde, whose personality is essentially evil, defends his artistic principles on the ground that he must needs express his personality, that art is nothing but such personal expression, and that it is subject to no standard save the individuality of the artist. Some writers on education, among them Mr. Bernard Shaw, who has many points in common with the Sophists, tell us that to attempt to mould the character of a child by discipline, is to sin against its personality, and that the child should be allowed to develop its individuality unchecked in its own way. But against this we have to protest that to make the cultivation of individuality an end in itself, and to put exclusive emphasis on this, is wrong. The cultivation of an individuality is not in itself a good thing; it is not a good thing if the individuality be a worthless one. If a child exhibits savage or selfish tendencies, it must be subjected to discipline, and it is ridiculous to make a fetish of its personality to such an extent as to allow it to develop as it likes. In a similar way, the ideal of individuality is often interpreted to mean that the cultivation of the mere eccentricities and oddities of the individual is something good. But the personal peculiarities of a man are just what is worthless about him. That alone which entitles him to the sacred rights of a "person" is his rational and universal nature.

CHAPTER X
SOCRATES

Amid the destruction of all ideals of truth and morality, which was brought about by the Sophists, there appeared in Athens the figure of Socrates, who was destined to restore order out of chaos, and to introduce sanity into the disordered intellectual life of the time. Socrates was born about 470 B.C. in Athens. His father was a sculptor, his mother a midwife. Very little is known of his early years and education, except that he took up his father's occupation as a sculptor. In later years some statues used to be shown at the Acropolis in Athens, which were said to be the work of Socrates. But comparatively early in life he deserted his profession in order to devote himself to what he considered his mission in life, philosophy. He spent his entire life in Athens, never departing from it, save for short periods on three occasions, when he served in military expeditions in the Athenian army. For from twenty to thirty years he laboured at his philosophical mission in Athens, until, in his seventieth year, he was charged with denying the national gods, introducing new gods of his own, and corrupting the Athenian youth. On these charges he was condemned to death and executed.

The personal appearance of Socrates was grotesque. He was short, thick-set, and ugly. As he grew older he became bald; his nose was broad, flat, and turned up; he walked with a peculiar gait, and had a trick of rolling his eyes. His clothes were old and poor. He cared little or nothing for external appearances.

Socrates believed that he was guided in all his actions by a supernatural voice, which he called his "daemon." This voice, he thought, gave him premonitions of the good or evil consequences of his proposed actions, and nothing would induce him to disobey its injunctions. Socrates constructed no philosophy, that is to say, no system of philosophy. He was the author of philosophical tendencies, and of a philosophic method. He never committed his opinions to writing. His method of philosophizing was purely conversational. It was his habit to go down every day to the market place in Athens, or to any other spot where people gathered, and there to engage in conversation with anyone who was ready to talk to him about the deep problems of life and death. Rich or poor, young or old, friend or stranger, whoever came, and would attend, could listen freely to the talk of Socrates. He took no fees, as the Sophists did, and remained always a poor man. He did not, like the Sophists, deliver long speeches, tirades, and monologues. He never monopolised the conversation, and frequently it was the other party who did most of the talking, Socrates only interposing questions and comments, and yet remaining always master of the conversation, and directing it into fruitful channels. The conversation proceeded chiefly by the method of question and answer, Socrates by acute questions educing, bringing to birth, the thoughts of his partner, correcting, refuting, or developing them.

In carrying on this daily work, Socrates undoubtedly regarded himself as engaged upon a mission in some way supernaturally imposed upon him by God. Of the origin of this mission we have an account in the "Apology" of Plato, who puts into the mouth of Socrates the following words:-- "Chairephon .... made a pilgrimage to Delphi and had the audacity to ask this question from the oracle .... He actually asked if there was any man wiser than I. And the priestess answered, No .... When I heard the answer, I asked myself: What can the god mean? what can he be hinting? For certainly I have never thought myself wise in anything, great or small. What can he mean then, when he asserts that I am the wisest of men? He cannot lie, of course: that would be impossible for him. And for a long while I was at a loss to think what he could mean. At last, after much thought, I started on some such course as this. I betook myself to one of the men who seemed wise, thinking that there, if anywhere, I should refute the utterance, and could say to the oracle: 'This man is wiser than I, and you said I was the wisest.' Now when I looked into the man--there is no need to give his name--it was one of our citizens, men of Athens, with whom I had an experience of this kind--when we talked together I thought, 'This man seems wise to many men, and above all to himself, but he is not so'; and then I tried to show that he thought he was wise, but he was not. Then he got angry with me and so did many who heard us, but I went away and thought to myself, 'Well, at any rate I am wiser than this man: probably neither of us knows anything of beauty or of good, but he thinks he knows something when he knows nothing, and I, if I know nothing, at least never suppose that I do. So it looks as though I really were a little wiser than he, just in so far as I do not imagine myself to know things about which I know nothing at all.' After that I went to another man who seemed to be wiser still, and I had exactly the same experience, and then he got angry with me too, and so did many more. Thus I went round them all, one after the other, aware of what was happening and sorry for it, and afraid that they were getting to hate me."

In this passage we can see, too, the supposed origin of another peculiar Socratic feature, the Socratic "irony." In any discussion, Socrates would, as a rule, profess himself to be totally ignorant of the matter in hand, and only anxious to learn the wisdom possessed by his interlocutor. This professed ignorance was not affectation. He was genuinely impressed with the notion that not only he, but all other men, live for the most part in ignorance of the things that are the most important to be known, the nature of goodness, beauty, and truth. He believed that the self-styled knowledge of the wise was, for the most part, nothing but pretentious ignorance. Nevertheless, he used this profession of ignorance as a weapon of offence, and it became in his hands a powerful rhetorical instrument, which he used with specially telling effect against those who, puffed up with their own importance and wisdom, pretended to knowledge which they did not possess. Such hollow pretence of knowledge met with uncompromising exposure at the hands of Socrates. With such persons he would open the conversation with a confession of his own ignorance and an expression of his desire to learn the wisdom, which, he knew, they possessed. In their eagerness to show off their knowledge, they would, perhaps, rush into the breach with some very positive assertion. Socrates would express himself as delighted with this, but would add that there were one or two things about it which he did not fully understand, and he would proceed, with a few dexterous questions, to expose the hollowness, the shallowness, or the ignorance of the answers.

It was chiefly the young men of Athens who gathered round Socrates, who was for them a centre of intellectual activity and a fountain of inspiration. It was this fact which afterwards formed the basis of the charge that he "corrupted the youth." He was a man of the noblest character and of the simplest life. Accepting no fees, he acquired no wealth. Poor, caring nothing for worldly goods, wholly independent of the ordinary needs and desires of men, he devoted himself exclusively to the acquisition of that which, in his eyes, alone had value, wisdom and virtue. He was endowed with the utmost powers of physical endurance and moral strength. When he served with the army in the Peloponnesian war, he astonished his fellow-soldiers by his bravery, and his cheerful endurance of every hardship. On two occasions, at considerable risk to himself, he saved the lives of his companions. At the battle of Delium it is said that Socrates was the only man who kept his head in the rout of the Athenians. He was an excellent companion, and though simple in his habits, and independent of all material pleasures, never made a fetish of this independence, nor allowed it to degenerate into a harsh asceticism, Thus, he needed no wine, but yet, if occasion called for it, he not only drank, but could drink more than any other man without turning a hair. In the "Banquet" of Plato, Socrates is depicted sitting all night long drinking and talking philosophy with his friends. One by one the guests succumbed, leaving only Socrates and two others, and at last, as the dawn broke, these two also fell asleep. But Socrates got up, washed himself, and went down to the market place to begin his daily work.

In his seventieth year he was tried on three charges: (1) for denying the national gods, (2) for setting up new gods of his own, (3) for corrupting the youth. All these charges were entirely baseless. The first might well have been brought against almost any of the earlier Greek thinkers with some justice. Most of them disbelieved in the national religion; many of them openly denied the existence of the gods. Socrates, almost alone, had refrained from any such attitude. On the contrary, he always enjoined veneration towards the gods, and urged his hearers, in whatever city they might be, to honour the gods according to the custom of that city. According to Xenophon, however, he distinguished between the many gods and the one creator of the universe, who controls, guides, and guards over the lives of men. The second charge appears to have been based upon the claim of Socrates to be guided by a supernatural inner voice, but whatever we may think of this claim, it can hardly constitute good ground for a charge of introducing new gods. The third charge, that of corrupting the youth, was equally baseless, though the fact that Alcibiades, who had been a favourite pupil of Socrates, afterwards turned traitor to Athens, and led, moreover, a dissolute and unprincipled life, no doubt prejudiced the philosopher in the eyes of the Athenians. But Socrates was not responsible for the misdeeds of Alcibiades, and his general influence upon the Athenian youth was the very opposite of corrupting.

What then were the real reasons for these accusations? In the first place, there is no doubt that Socrates had made many personal enemies. In his daily disputations he had not spared even the most powerful men in Athens, but had ruthlessly laid bare the ignorance of those who pretended to be wise. There is, however, no reason to believe that the three men who actually laid the charges, Melitus, Lycon, and Anytus, did so out of any personal animosity. But they were men of straw, put forward by more powerful persons who remained behind the scenes. In the second place, Socrates had rendered himself obnoxious to the Athenian democracy. He was no aristocrat in feeling, nor was he a supporter of the vested interests and privileges of the few. But he could not accommodate himself to the mob-rule which then went by the name of democracy. The government of the State, he believed, should be in the hands of the wise, the just, and the good, those competent and trained to govern, and these are necessarily the few. He himself had taken no part in the political life of the time, preferring to guide by his influence and advice the young men on whom some day the duties of the State would devolve. On two occasions only did he take an active part in politics, and on both occasions his conduct gave great offence. Both these incidents are recounted in a passage in Plato's "Apology," which I will quote. The first incident refers to the aftermath of the battle of Arginusae. The Athenian fleet had gained a victory here, but lost twenty-five ships of war, and the whole of the crews of these ships were drowned. This was attributed to the carelessness of the generals, and there was great indignation in Athens, upon their return whither the generals were put upon their trial. According to the law of Athens each accused had to be given a separate trial, but in their eagerness to have the generals condemned, the judges in this instance decided to try them all in a body. "You know, men of Athens," says Socrates in the "Apology," "that I have never held any other office in the State, but I did serve on the Council. And it happened that my tribe, Antiochis, had the Presidency at the time you decided to try the ten generals who had not taken up the dead after the fight at sea. You decided to try them in one body, contrary to law, as you all felt afterwards. On that occasion I was the only one of the Presidents who opposed you, and told you not to break the law; and I gave my vote against you; and when the orators were ready to impeach and arrest me, and you encouraged them and hooted me, I thought then that I ought to take all the risks on the side of law and justice, rather than side with you, when your decisions were unjust, through fear of imprisonment or death. That was while the city was still under the democracy. When the oligarchy came into power, the Thirty, in their turn, summoned me with four others to the Rotunda, and commanded us to fetch Leon of Salamis from that island, in order to put him to death: the sort of commands they often gave to many others, anxious as they were to incriminate all they could. And on that occasion I showed not by words only, that for death, to put it bluntly, I did not care one straw--but I did care, and to the full, about doing what was wicked and unjust. I was not terrified then into doing wrong by that government in all its power; when we left the Rotunda, the other four went off to Salamis and brought Leon back, but I went home. And probably I should have been put to death for it, if the government had not been overthrown soon afterwards."

But there was a third, and greater reason, for the condemnation of Socrates. These charges were brought against him because the popular mind confused him with the Sophists. This was entirely absurd, because Socrates in no respect resembled the Sophists, either in the manner of his life or in the tendency of his thought, which was wholly anti-sophistical. But that such a confusion did exist in the popular mind is clearly proved by "The Clouds" of Aristophanes. Aristophanes was a reactionary in thought and politics, and, hating the Sophists as the representatives of modernism, he lampooned them in his comedy, "The Clouds." Socrates appears in the play as the central character, and the chief of the Sophists. This was entirely unjust, but it affords evidence of the fact that Socrates was commonly mistaken for a Sophist by the Athenians. Aristophanes would not have ventured to introduce such a delusion into his play, had his audience not shared in it. Now at this time a wave of reaction was passing over Athens, and there was great indignation against the Sophists, who were rightly supposed to be overturning all ideals of truth and goodness. Socrates fell a victim to the anger of the populace against the Sophists.

At the trial Socrates conducted himself with dignity and confidence. It was usual in those days for an accused person to weep and lament, to flatter the judges, to seek indulgence by grovelling and fawning, to appeal for pity by parading his wife and children in the court. Socrates refused to do any of these things, considering them unmanly. His "defence" was, indeed, not so much a defence of himself as an arraignment of his judges, the people of Athens, for their corruption and vice. This attitude of Socrates certainly brought about his condemnation. There is every reason to believe that if he had adopted a grovelling, even a conciliatory tone, he would have been acquitted. As it was, he was found guilty by a bare majority. The law enacted that, when the charge was proved, those who had brought the accusation should first propose the penalty which they thought fitting; then the accused himself should propose an alternative penalty. It was for the judges to decide which of the two should be inflicted. The accusers of Socrates proposed the death-penalty. Here again Socrates might have escaped by proposing at once some petty punishment. This would have satisfied the people, who were only anxious to score off the troublesome philosopher and pedant. But Socrates proudly affirmed that, as he was guilty of no crime, he deserved no punishment. To propose a penalty would be to admit his guilt. Far from being a guilty person, he considered himself in the light of a public benefactor, and as such, if he were to get his deserts, he proposed that he should be publicly honoured by being given a seat at the President's table. Nevertheless, as the law forced him to propose a penalty, he would, without prejudice to his plea of innocence, suggest a fine of thirty minas. This conduct so exasperated the judges that he was now condemned to death by a large majority, about eighty of those who had previously voted for his acquittal now voting for his execution.

Thirty days elapsed before he was executed, and these days were spent in prison. His friends, who had free access to him, urged him to escape. These things were possible in Athens. Anaxagoras had apparently escaped with the help of Pericles. A little silver in the hands of the jailguards would probably have settled the matter. Socrates could fly to Thessaly, where the law could not reach him, as Anaxagoras had fled to Ionia. But Socrates steadily refused, saying that to flee from death was cowardly, and that one ought to obey the laws. The law had decreed his death, and he must obey. After thirty days, therefore, the poison cup was brought to him, and he drank it without flinching. Here is Plato's account of the death of Socrates, which I quote from the "Phaedo." In detail it cannot be considered historical, but we may well believe that the main incidents as well as the picture it gives us of the bearing and demeanour of the philosopher in his last moments, are accurate representations of the facts.

"He rose and went into a chamber to bathe, and Crito followed him, but he directed us to wait for him. We waited, therefore, conversing among ourselves about what had been said, and considering it again, and sometimes speaking about our calamity, how severe it would be to us, sincerely thinking that, like those who are deprived of a father, we should pass the rest of our lives as orphans. When he had bathed and his children were brought to him, for he had two little sons and one grown up, and the women belonging to his family were come, having conversed with them in the presence of Crito, and given them such injunctions as he wished, he directed the women and children to go away, and then returned to us. And it was now near sunset; for he spent a considerable time within. But when he came from bathing he sat down and did not speak much afterwards: then the officer of the Eleven came in and standing near him said, 'Socrates, I shall not have to find that fault with you that I do with the others, that they are angry with me, and curse me, when, by order of the archons, I bid them drink the poison. But you, on all other occasions during the time you have been here, I have found to be the most noble, meek and excellent man of all that ever came into this place; and, therefore, I am now well convinced that you will not be angry with me. Now, then, for you know what I came to announce to you, farewell, and endeavour to bear what is inevitable as easily as possible.' And at the same time, bursting into tears, he turned away and withdrew. And Socrates, looking after him, said, 'And thou too, farewell, we will do as you direct.' At the same time, turning to us he said 'How courteous the man is; during the whole time I have been here he has visited me, and conversed with me sometimes, and proved the worthiest of men; and how generously he weeps for me. But come, Crito, let us obey him and let some one bring the poison, if it is ready pounded, but if not let the man pound it.'

"Then Crito said, 'But I think, Socrates, that the sun is still on the mountains, and has not yet set. Besides, I know that others have drunk the poison very late, after it had been announced to them, and have supped and drunk freely, and some even have enjoyed the objects of their love. Do not hasten them, for there is yet time.'

"Upon this Socrates replied, 'These men whom you mention, Crito, do these things with good reason, for they think they shall gain by so doing, and I too with good reason, shall not do so; for I think I shall gain nothing by drinking a little later, except to become ridiculous to myself, in being so fond of life, and sparing of it when none any longer remains. Go then,' he said, 'obey, and do not resist.'

"Crito having heard this, nodded to the boy that stood near. And the boy having gone out, and stayed for some time, came, bringing with him the man that was to administer the poison, who brought it ready pounded in a cup. And Socrates, on seeing the man, said, 'Well, my good friend, as you are skilled in these matters, what must I do?' 'Nothing else,' he replied, 'than when you have drunk it walk about, until there is a heaviness in your legs, then lie down; thus it will do its purpose.' And at the same time he held out the cup to Socrates. And he having received it very cheerfully, Echecrates, neither trembling, nor changing at all in colour or countenance, but, as he was wont, looking steadfastly at the man, said, 'what say you of this potion, with respect to making a libation to anyone, is it lawful or not?'

'We only pound so much, Socrates,' he said, 'as we think sufficient to drink.' 'I understand you,' he said, 'but it is certainly both lawful and right to pray to the gods that my departure hence thither may be happy; which therefore I pray, and so may it be.' And as he said this he drank it off readily and calmly. Thus far, most of us were with difficulty able to restrain ourselves from weeping, but when we saw him drinking, and having finished the draught, we could do so no longer; but in spite of myself the tears came in full torrent, so that, covering my face, I wept for myself, for I did not weep for him, but for my own fortune, in being deprived of such a friend. But Crito, even before me, when he could not restrain his tears, had risen up. But Apollodorus even before this had not ceased weeping, and then, bursting into an agony of grief, weeping and lamenting, he pierced the heart of everyone present, except Socrates himself. But he said. 'What are you doing, my admirable friends? I indeed, for this reason chiefly, sent away the women, that they might not commit any folly of this kind. For I have heard that it is right to die with good omens. Be quiet, therefore, and bear up.'

"When we heard this we were ashamed, and restrained our tears. But he, having walked about, when he said that his legs were growing heavy, lay down on his back; for the man so directed him. And at the same time he who gave him the poison, taking hold of him, after a short interval examined his feet and legs; and then having pressed his foot hard, he asked if he felt it; he said that he did not. And after this he pressed his thighs; and thus going higher he showed us that he was growing cold and stiff. Then Socrates touched himself, and said that when the poison reached his heart he should then depart. But now the parts around the lower belly were almost cold; when uncovering himself, for he had been covered over, he said; and they were his last words. 'Crito, we owe a cock to AEsculapius; pay it, therefore, and do not neglect it.' 'It shall be done,' said Crito, 'but consider whether you have anything else to say.'

"To this question he gave no reply; but shortly after he gave a convulsive movement, and the man covered him, and his eyes were fixed, and Crito, perceiving it, closed his mouth and eyes.

"This, Echecrates, was the end of our friend, a man, as we may say, the best of all of his time that we have known, and moreover, the most wise and just."

Our knowledge of the teaching of Socrates is derived chiefly from two sources, Plato and Xenophon, for the peculiarities of each of whom allowances must be made. Plato in his dialogues makes Socrates the mouthpiece of his own teaching, consequently the majority of the tenets to which Socrates is made to give expression are purely Platonic doctrines of which the historical Socrates could never even have dreamed. It might, therefore, seem at first sight that there is no possibility of ascertaining from Plato's dialogues any trustworthy account of the ideas of Socrates. But on closer inspection this does not turn out to be correct, because the earlier dialogues of Plato were written before he had developed his own philosophy, and when he was, to all intents and purposes, simply a disciple of Socrates, bent only upon giving the best expression to the Socratic doctrine. Even in these Socratic dialogues, however, we have what is no doubt an idealized portrait of Socrates. Plato makes no pretence of being merely a biographer or historian. The incidents and conversation, although they are no doubt frequently founded upon facts, are, in the main, imaginary. All we can say is that they contain the gist and substance of the philosophy of Socrates. The other source, Xenophon, also has his peculiarities. If Plato was an idealizing philosopher, Xenophon was a prosaic and matter of fact man of affairs. He was a plain, honest soldier. He had no great insight into any philosophy, Socratic or otherwise. He was not attached to Socrates primarily as a philosopher, but as an admirer of his character and personality. If Plato puts the teaching of Socrates too high, Xenophon puts it too low. But, in spite of this, Xenophon's Memorabilia contains a mass of valuable information both about the life and the philosophical ideas of Socrates.

The Socratic teaching is essentially ethical in character. In this alone did Socrates bear any resemblance to the Sophists. It was the Sophists who had introduced into Greek philosophy the problem of man, and of the duties of man. And to these problems Socrates also turns his exclusive attention. He brushes aside all questions as to the origin of the world, or the nature of the ultimate reality, of which we have heard so much in the philosophies of the earlier thinkers. Socrates openly deprecated such speculations and considered all such knowledge comparatively worthless as against ethical knowledge, the knowledge of man. Mathematics, physics, and astronomy, he thought, were not valuable forms of knowledge. He said that he never went for walks outside the city, because there is nothing to be learnt from fields and trees.

Nevertheless the ethical teaching of Socrates was founded upon a theory of knowledge, which is quite simple, but extremely important. The Sophists had founded knowledge upon perception, with the result that all objective standards of truth had been destroyed. It was the work of Socrates to found knowledge upon reason, and thereby to restore to truth its objectivity. Briefly, the theory of Socrates may be summarized by saying that he taught that all knowledge is knowledge through concepts. What is a concept? When we are directly conscious of the presence of any particular thing, a man, a tree, a house, or a star, such consciousness is called perception. When, shutting our eyes, we frame a mental picture of such an object, such consciousness is called an image or representation. Such mental images are, like perceptions, always ideas of particular individual objects. But besides these ideas of individual objects, whether through sense-perception or imagination, we have also general ideas, that is to say, not ideas of any particular thing, but ideas of whole classes of things. If I say "Socrates is mortal," I am thinking of the individual, Socrates. But if I say "Man is mortal," I am thinking, not of any particular man, but of the class of men in general. Such an idea is called a general idea, or a concept. All class-names, such as man, tree, house, river, animal, horse, being, which stand, not for one thing, but for a multitude of things, represent concepts. We form these general ideas by including in them all the qualities which the whole class of objects has in common, and excluding from them all the qualities in which they differ, that is to say, the qualities which some of the objects possess, but others do not. For example, I cannot include the quality whiteness in my general idea of horses, because, though some horses are white, others are not. But I can include the quality vertebrate because all horses agree in being vertebrate. Thus a concept is formed by bringing together the ideas in which all the members of a class of objects agree with one another, and neglecting the ideas in which they differ.

Now reason is the faculty of concepts. This may not, at first sight, be obvious. Reason, it might be objected, is the faculty of arguing, of drawing conclusions from premises. But a little consideration will show us that, though this is so, yet all reasoning is employed upon concepts. All reasoning is either deductive or inductive. Induction consists in the formulation of general principles from particular cases. A general principle is always a statement made, not about a particular thing, but about a whole class of things, that is, about a concept. Concepts are formed inductively by comparing numerous examples of a class. Deductive reasoning is always the opposite process of applying general principles to particular cases. If we argue that Socrates must be mortal because all men are so, the question is whether Socrates is a man, that is to say, whether the concept, man, is properly applied to the particular object called Socrates. Thus inductive reasoning is concerned with the formation of concepts, deductive reasoning with the application of them.

Socrates, in placing all knowledge in concepts, was thus making reason the organ of knowledge. This was in direct opposition to the principle of the Sophists, who placed all knowledge in sense-perception. Now since reason is the universal element in man, it follows that Socrates, in identifying knowledge with concepts, was restoring the belief in an objective truth, valid for all men, and binding upon all men, and was destroying the Sophistic teaching that the truth is whatever each individual chooses to think it is. We shall see this more clearly if we reflect that a concept is the same thing as a definition. If we wish to define any word, for example, the word man, we must include in our definition only the qualities which all men have in common. We cannot, for example, define man as a white-skinned animal, because all men are not white-skinned. Similarly we cannot include "English-speaking" in our definition, because, though some men speak English, others do not. But we might include such a quality as "two-legged," because "two-legged" is a quality common to all human beings, except mere aberrations and distortions of the normal type. Thus a definition is formed in the same way as a concept, namely, by including the common qualities of a class of objects, and excluding the qualities in which the members of the class differ. A definition, in fact, is merely the expression of a concept in words. Now by the process of fixing definitions we obtain objective standards of truth. If, for example, we fix the definition of a triangle, then we can compare any geometrical figure with it, and say whether it is a triangle or not. It is no longer open to anyone to declare that whatever he chooses to call a triangle is a triangle. Similarly, if we fix upon a definition of the word man, we can then compare any object with that definition, and say whether it is a man or not. Again, if we can decide what the proper concept of virtue is, then the question whether any particular act is virtuous can only be decided by comparing that act with the concept, and seeing if they agree. The Sophist can no longer say, "whatever seems to me right, is right for me. Whatever I choose to do is virtuous for me." His act must be judged, not by his subjective impressions, but by the concept or definition, which is thus an objective standard of truth, independent of the individual. This, then, was the theory of knowledge propounded by Socrates. Knowledge, he said, is not the same thing as the sensations of the individual, which would mean that each individual can name as the truth whatever he pleases. Knowledge means knowledge of things as they objectively are, independently of the individual, and such knowledge is knowledge of the concepts of things. Therefore the philosophizing of Socrates consisted almost exclusively in trying to frame proper concepts. He went about enquiring, "What is virtue?" "What is prudence?" "What is temperance?"--meaning thereby "what are the true concepts or definitions of these things?" In this way he attempted to find a basis for believing in an objectively real truth and an objectively real moral law.

His method of forming concepts was by induction. He would take common examples of actions which are universally admitted to be prudent, and would attempt to find the quality which they all have in common, and by virtue of which they are all classed together, and so form the concept of prudence. Then he would bring up fresh examples, and see whether they agreed with the concept so formed. If not, the concept might have to be corrected in the light of the new examples.

But the Socratic theory of knowledge was not a theory put forward for its own sake, but for practical ends. Socrates always made theory subservient to practice. He wanted to know what the concept of virtue is, only in order to practise virtue in life. And this brings us to the central point of the ethical teaching of Socrates, which was the identification of virtue with knowledge. Socrates believed that a man cannot act rightly, unless he first knows what is right, unless, in fact, he knows the concept of right. Moral action is thus founded upon knowledge, and must spring from it. But not only did Socrates think that if a man has not knowledge, he cannot do right. He also put forward the much more doubtful assertion that if a man possesses knowledge, he cannot do wrong. All wrong-doing arises from ignorance. If a man only knows what is right, he must and will infallibly do what is right. All men seek the good, but men differ as to what the good is. "No man," said Socrates, "intentionally does wrong." He does wrong, because he does not know the true concept of right, and being ignorant, thinks that what he is doing is good. "If a man intentionally does wrong," said Socrates again, "he is better than a man who does so unintentionally." For the former has in him the essential condition of goodness, knowledge of what goodness is, but the latter, lacking that knowledge, is hopeless.

Aristotle, in commenting upon this whole doctrine, observed that Socrates had ignored or forgotten the irrational parts of the soul. Socrates imagined that everybody's actions are governed solely by reason, and that therefore if only they reasoned aright, they must do right. He forgot that the majority of men's actions are governed by passions and emotions, "the irrational parts of the soul." Aristotle's criticism of Socrates is unanswerable. All experience shows that men do deliberately do wrong, that, knowing well what is right, they nevertheless do wrong. But it is easy to see why Socrates made this mistake; he was arguing only from his own case. Socrates really does appear to have been above human weakness. He was not guided by passions, but by reason, and it followed as the night follows the day, that if Socrates knew what was right, he did it. He was unable to understand how men, knowing the right, could yet do the wrong. If they are vicious, he thought, it must be because they do not know what is right. The criticism of Aristotle is thus justified. Yet for all that, the theory of Socrates is not to be too quickly brushed aside. There is more truth in it than appears at first sight. We say that a man believes one thing and does another. Yet it is a matter of question what a man really believes, and what is the test of his belief. Men go to church every Sunday, and there repeat formulas and prayers, of which the main idea is that all earthly riches are worthless in comparison with spiritual treasures. Such men, if asked, might tell us that they believe this to be true. They believe that they believe it. And yet in actual life, perhaps, they seek only for earthly riches, and behave as if they thought these the supreme good. What do such men really believe? Do they believe as they speak, or as they act? Is it not at least arguable that they are really pursuing what they believe to be good, and that, if they were genuinely convinced of the superiority of spiritual treasures, they would seek them, and not material riches? This at least is what Socrates thought. All men seek the good, but the many do not know what the good is. There is certainly truth in this in many cases, though in others there can be no doubt that men do deliberately what they know to be evil.

There are two other characteristic Socratic propositions which flow from the same general idea, that virtue is identical with knowledge. The first is, that virtue can be taught. We do not ordinarily think that virtue can be taught like arithmetic. We think that virtue depends upon a number of factors, prominent among which are the inborn disposition of a man, heredity, environment, modified to some extent by education, practice, and habit. The consequence is that a man's character does not change very much as he grows older. By constant practice, by continual self-control, a man may, to some extent, make himself better, but on the whole, what he is he remains. The leopard, we say, does not change his spots. But as, for Socrates, the sole condition of virtue is knowledge, and as knowledge is just what can be imparted by teaching, it followed that virtue must be teachable. The only difficulty is to find the teacher, to find some one who knows the concept of virtue. What the concept of virtue is--that is, thought Socrates, the precious piece of knowledge, which no philosopher has ever discovered, and which, if it were only discovered, could at once be imparted by teaching, whereupon men would at once become virtuous.

The other Socraticism is that "virtue is one." We talk of many virtues, temperance, prudence, foresight, benevolence, kindness, etc. Socrates believed that all these particular virtues flowed from the one source, knowledge. Therefore knowledge itself, that is to say, wisdom, is the sole virtue, and this includes all the others.

This completes the exposition of the positive teaching of Socrates. It only remains for us to consider what position Socrates holds in the history of thought. There are two sides of the Socratic teaching. In the first place, there is the doctrine of knowledge, that all knowledge is through concepts. This is the scientific side of the philosophy of Socrates. Secondly, there is his ethical teaching. Now the essential and important side of Socrates is undoubtedly the scientific theory of concepts. It is this which gives him his position in the history of philosophy. His ethical ideas, suggestive as they were, were yet all tainted with the fallacy that men are governed only by reason. Hence they have exercised no great influence on the history of thought. But the theory of concepts worked a revolution in philosophy. Upon a development of it is founded the whole of Plato's philosophy, and, through Plato, the philosophy of Aristotle, and, indeed, all subsequent idealism. The immediate effect of this theory, however, was the destruction of the teaching of the Sophists. The Sophists taught the doctrine that truth is sense-perception, and as the perceptions of different individuals differ in regard to the same object, it followed that truth became a matter of taste with the individual. This undermined all belief in truth as an objective reality, and, by similar reasoning, faith in the objectivity of the moral law was also destroyed. The essential position of Socrates is that of a restorer of faith. His greatness lay in the fact that he saw that the only way to combat the disastrous results of the Sophistic teaching was to refute the fundamental assumption from which all that teaching flowed, the assumption, namely, that knowledge is perception. Against this, therefore, Socrates opposed the doctrine that knowledge is through concepts. To base knowledge upon concepts is to base it upon the universality of reason, and therefore to restore it from the position of a subjective seeming to that of an objective reality.

But though Socrates is thus a restorer of faith, we must not imagine that his thought is therefore a mere retrogression to the intellectual condition of pre-Sophistic times. It was, on the contrary, an advance beyond the Sophists. We have here, in fact, an example of what is the normal development of all thought, whether in the individual or the race. The movement of thought exhibits three stages. The first stage is positive belief, not founded upon reason; it is merely conventional belief. At the second stage thought becomes destructive and sceptical. It denies what was affirmed in the previous stage. The third stage is the restoration of positive belief now founded upon the concept, upon reason, and not merely upon custom. Before the time of the Sophists, men took it for granted that truth and goodness are objective realities; nobody specially affirmed it, because nobody denied it. It seemed obvious. It was, thus, not believed on rational grounds, but through custom and habit. This, the first stage of thought, we may call the era of simple faith. When the Sophists came upon the scene, they brought reason and thought to bear upon what had hitherto been accepted as a matter of course, namely law, custom, and authority. The first encroachment of reason upon simple faith is always destructive, and hence the Sophists undermined all ideals of goodness and truth. Socrates is the restorer of these ideals, but with him they are no longer the ideals of simple faith; they are the ideals of reason. They are based upon reason. Socrates substituted comprehending belief for unintelligent assent. We may contrast him, in this respect, with Aristophanes. Aristophanes, the conservative, the believer in the "good old times," saw, as clearly as Socrates, the disastrous effects worked by the Sophists upon public morals. But the remedy he proposed was a violent return to the "good old times." Since it was thought which worked these ill effects, thought must be suppressed. We must go back to simple faith. But simple faith, once destroyed by thought, never returns either to the individual, or to the race. This can no more happen than a man can again become a child. There is only one remedy for the ills of thought, and that is, more thought. If thought, in its first inroads, leads, as it always does, to scepticism and denial, the only course is, not to suppress thought, but to found faith upon it. This was the method of Socrates, and it is the method, too, of all great spirits. They are not frightened of shadows. They have faith in reason. If reason leads them into the darkness, they do not scuttle back in fright. They advance till the light comes again. They are false teachers who counsel us to give no heed to the promptings of reason, if reason brings doubt into our beliefs. Thought cannot be thus suppressed. Reason has rights upon us as rational beings. We cannot go back. We must go on, and make our beliefs rational. We must found them upon the concept, as Socrates did. Socrates did not deny the principle of the Sophists that all institutions, all ideals, all existing and established things must justify themselves before the tribunal of reason. He accepted this without question. He took up the challenge of thought, and won the battle of reason in his day.

The Sophists brought to light the principle of subjectivity, the principle that the truth must be my truth, and the right my right. They must be the products of my own thinking, not standards forcibly imposed upon me from without. But the mistake of the Sophists was to imagine that the truth must be mine, merely in my capacity as a percipient creature of sense, which means that I have a private truth of my own. Socrates corrected this by admitting that the truth must be my truth, but mine in my capacity as a rational being, which means, since reason is the universal, that it is not my private truth, but universal truth which is shared by and valid for all rational beings. Truth is thus established as being not mere subjective appearance, but objective reality, independent of the sensations, whims, and self-will of the individual. The whole period of Socrates and the Sophists is full of instruction. Its essential lesson is that to deny the supremacy of reason, to set up any other process of consciousness above reason, must inevitably end in scepticism and the denial of the objectivity of truth and morality. Many theosophists and others, at the present day, teach the doctrine of what they call "intuition." The supreme kind of religious knowledge, they think, is to be reached by intuition, which is conceived as something higher than reason. But this is simply to make the mistake of Protagoras over again. It is true that this so-called intuition is not merely sense-perception, as was the case with Protagoras. It is, however, a form of immediate spiritual perception. It is immediate apprehension of the object as being present to me, as having thereness. It is therefore of the nature of perception. It is spiritual and super-sensuous, as opposed to material and sensuous, perception. But it makes no difference at all whether perception is sensuous or super-sensuous. To place the truth in any sort of perception is, in principle, to do as Protagoras did, to yield oneself up a helpless prey to the subjective impressions of the individual. I intuit one thing; another man intuits the opposite. What I intuit must be true for me, what he intuits true for him. For we have denied reason, we have placed it below intuition, and have thereby discarded that which alone can subject the varying impressions of each individual to the rule of a universal and objective standard. The logical conclusion is that, since each man's intuition is true for him, there is no such thing as an objective truth. Nor can there be such a thing, in these circumstances, as an objective goodness. Thus the theory must end in total scepticism and darkness. The fact that theosophists do not, as a matter of fact, draw these sceptical conclusions, simply means that they are not as clear-headed and logical as Protagoras was.

CHAPTER XI
THE SEMI-SOCRATICS

Upon the death of Socrates there ensued a phenomenon which is not infrequent in the history of thought. A great and many-sided personality combines in himself many conflicting tendencies and ideas. Let us take an example, not, however, from the sphere of intellect, but from the sphere of practical life. We often say that it is difficult to reconcile mercy and justice. Among the many small personalities, one man follows only the ideal of mercy, and as his mercy has not in it the stern stuff of justice, it degenerates into mawkishness and sentimental humanitarianism. Another man follows only the ideal of justice, forgetting mercy, and he becomes harsh and unsympathetic. It takes a greater man, a larger personality, harmoniously to combine the two. And as it is in the sphere of practical life, so it is in the arena of thought and philosophy. A great thinker is not he who seizes upon a single aspect of the truth, and pushes that to its extreme limit, but the man who combines, in one many-sided system, all the varying and conflicting sides of truth. By emphasizing one thought, by being obsessed by a single idea and pushing it to its logical conclusion, regardless of the other aspects of the truth, one may indeed achieve a considerable local and temporary reputation; because such a procedure often leads to striking paradoxes, to strange and seemingly uncommon conclusions. The reputations of such men as Nietzsche, Bernard Shaw, Oscar Wilde, are made chiefly in this way. But upon the death of a great all-embracing personality, just because his thought is a combination of so many divergent truths, we often find that it splits up into its component parts, each of which gives rise to a one-sided school of thought. The disciples, being smaller men, are not able to grasp the great man's thought in its wholeness and many-sidedness. Each disciple seizes upon that portion of his master's teaching which has most in common with his own temperament, and proceeds to erect this one incomplete idea into a philosophy, treating the part as if it were the whole. This is exactly what happened after the death of Socrates. Only one man among his disciples was able to grasp the whole of his teaching, and understand the whole of his personality, and that was Plato. Among the lesser men who were the followers and personal friends of Socrates, there were three who founded schools of philosophy, each partial and one-sided, but each claiming to be the exponent of the true Socraticism. Antisthenes founded the Cynic school, Aristippus the Cyrenaic, and Euclid the Megaric.

Now, of the two aspects of the Socratic philosophy, the theory of concepts, and the ethical theory, it is easy for us, looking back upon history, to see which it was that influenced the history of thought most, and which, therefore, was the most important. But the men of his own time could not see this. What they fastened upon was the obvious aspect of Socrates, his ethics, and above all the ethical teaching which was expressed, not so much in abstract ideas, as in the life and personality of the master. Both this life and this teaching might be summed up in the thought that virtue is the sole end of life, that, as against virtue, all else in the world, comfort, riches, learning, is comparatively worthless. It is this, then, that virtue is the sole end of life, which forms the point of agreement between all the three semi-Socratic schools. We have now to see upon what points they diverge from one another.

If virtue is the sole end of life, what precisely is virtue? Socrates had given no clear answer to this question. The only definition he had given was that virtue is knowledge, but upon examination it turns out that this is not a definition at all. Virtue is knowledge, but knowledge of what? It is not knowledge of astronomy, of mathematics, or of physics. It is ethical knowledge, that is to say, knowledge of virtue. To define virtue as the knowledge of virtue is to think in a circle, and gets us no further in the enquiry what virtue is. But Socrates, as a matter of fact, did not think in a circle. He did not mean that virtue is knowledge, although his doctrine is often, somewhat misleadingly, stated in that form. What he meant was--quite a different thing--that virtue depends upon knowledge. It is the first condition of virtue. The principle, accurately stated, is, not that virtue is the knowledge of virtue, which is thinking in a circle, but that virtue depends upon the knowledge of virtue, which is quite straight thinking. Only if you know what virtue is can you be virtuous. Hence we have not here any definition of virtue, or any attempt to define it. We are still left with the question, "what is virtue?" unanswered.

No doubt this was due in part to the unmethodical and unsystematic manner in which Socrates developed his thought, and this, in its turn, was due to his conversational style of philosophizing. For it is not possible to develop systematic thinking in the course of casual conversations. But in part, too, it was due to the very universality of the man's genius. He was broad enough to realize that it is not possible to tie down virtue in any single narrow formula, which shall serve as a practical receipt for action in all the infinitely various circumstances of life. So that, in spite of the fact that his whole principle lay in the method of definitions, Socrates, in fact, left his followers without any definition of the supreme concept of his philosophy, virtue. It was upon this point, therefore, that the followers of Socrates disagreed. They all agreed that virtue is the sole end of life, but they developed different ideas as to what sort of life is in fact virtuous.

The Cynics.

Antisthenes, the founder of the Cynic School, repeated the familiar propositions that virtue is founded upon knowledge, is teachable, and is one. But what aroused the admiration of Antisthenes was not Socrates, the man of intellect, the man of science, the philosopher, but Socrates, the man of independent character, who followed his own notions of right with complete indifference to the opinions of others. This independence was in fact merely a by-product of the Socratic life. Socrates had been independent of all earthly goods and possessions, caring neither for riches nor for applause, only because his heart was set upon a greater treasure, the acquisition of wisdom. Mere independence and indifference to the opinions of others were not for him ends in themselves. He did not make fetishes of them. But the Cynics interpreted his teaching to mean that the independence of earthly pleasures and possessions is in itself the end and object of life. This, in fact, was their definition of virtue, complete renunciation of everything that, for ordinary men, makes life worth living, absolute asceticism, and rigorous self-mortification. Socrates, again, thinking that the only knowledge of supreme value is ethical knowledge, had exhibited a tendency to disparage other kinds of knowledge. This trait the Cynics exaggerated into a contempt for all art and learning so great as frequently to amount to ignorance and boorishness. "Virtue is sufficient for happiness," said Antisthenes, "and for virtue nothing is requisite but the strength of a Socrates; it is a matter of action, and does not require many words, or much learning." The Cynic ideal of virtue is thus purely negative; it is the absence of all desire, freedom from all wants, complete independence of all possessions. Many of them refused to own houses or any dwelling place, and wandered about as vagrants and beggars. Diogenes, for the same reason, lived in a tub. Socrates, following single-heartedly what he knew to be good, cared nothing what the vulgar said. But this indifference to the opinion of others was, like his independence of possessions, not an end in itself. He did not interpret it to mean that he was wantonly to offend public opinion. But the Cynics, to show their indifference, flouted public opinion, and gave frequent and disgusting exhibitions of indecency.

Virtue, for the Cynics, is alone good. Vice is the only evil. Nothing else in the world is either good or bad. Everything else is "indifferent." Property, pleasure, wealth, freedom, comfort, even life itself, are not to be regarded as goods. Poverty, misery, illness, slavery, and death itself, are not to be regarded as evils. It is no better to be a freeman than a slave, for if the slave have virtue, he is in himself free, and a born ruler. Suicide is not a crime, and a man may destroy his life, not however to escape from misery and pain (for these are not ills), but to show that for him life is indifferent. And as the line between virtue and vice is absolutely definite, so is the distinction between the wise man and the fool. All men are divided into these two classes. There is no middle term between them. Virtue being one and indivisible, either a man possesses it whole or does not possess it at all. In the former case he is a wise man, in the latter case a fool. The wise man possesses all virtue, all knowledge, all wisdom, all happiness, all perfection. The fool possesses all evil, all misery, all imperfection.

The Cyrenaics.

For the Cyrenaics, too, virtue is, at least formally, the sole object of life. It is only formally, however, because they give to virtue a definition which robbed it of all meaning. Socrates had not infrequently recommended virtue on account of the advantages which it brings. Virtue, he said, is the sole path to happiness, and he had not refrained from holding out happiness as a motive for virtue. This did not mean, however, that he did not recognize a man's duty to do the right for its own sake, and not for the sake of the advantage it brings. "Honesty," we say, "is the best policy," but we do not mean thereby to deny that it is the duty of men to be honest even if it is not, in some particular case, the best policy. Socrates, however, had not been very clear upon these points, and had been unable to find any definite basis for morality, other than that of happiness. It was this side of his teaching which Aristippus now pressed to its logical conclusions, regardless of all other claims. Doubtless virtue is the sole end of life, but the sole end of virtue is one's own advantage, that is to say, pleasure. One may as well say at once that the sole end of life is pleasure.

The influence of Protagoras and the Sophists also played its part in moulding the thought of Aristippus. Protagoras had denied the objectivity of truth, and the later Sophists had applied the same theory to morals. Each man is a law unto himself. There is no moral code binding upon the individual against his own wishes. Aristippus combined this with his doctrine of pleasure. Pleasure being the sole end of life, no moral law externally imposed can invalidate its absolute claims. Nothing is wicked, nothing evil, provided only it satisfies the individual's thirst for pleasure.

Whether such a philosophy will lead, in practice, to the complete degradation of its devotees, depends chiefly upon what sort of pleasure they have in mind. If refined and intellectual pleasures are meant, there is no reason why a comparatively good life should not result. If bodily pleasures are intended, the results are not likely to be noble. The Cyrenaics by no means wholly ignored the pleasures of the mind, but they pointed out that feelings of bodily pleasure are more potent and intense, and it was upon these, therefore, that they chiefly concentrated their attention. Nevertheless they were saved from the lowest abysses of sensuality and bestiality by their doctrine that, in the pursuit of pleasure, the wise man must exercise prudence. Completely unrestrained pursuit of pleasure leads in fact to pain and disaster. Pain is that which has to be avoided. Therefore the wise man will remain always master of himself, will control his desires, and postpone a more urgent to a less urgent desire, if thereby in the end more pleasure and less pain will accrue to him. The Cyrenaic ideal of the wise man is the man of the world, bent indeed solely upon pleasure, restrained by no superstitious scruples, yet pursuing his end with prudence, foresight, and intelligence. Such principles would, of course, admit of various interpretations, according to the temperament of the individual. We may notice two examples. Anniceris, the Cyrenaic, believed indeed that pleasure is the sole end, but set such store upon the pleasures that arise from friendship and family affection, that he admitted that the wise man should be ready to sacrifice himself for his friends or family--a gleam of light in the moral darkness. Hegesias, a pessimist, considered that positive enjoyment is impossible of attainment. In practice the sole end of life which can be realized is the avoidance of pain.

The Megarics.

Euclid of Megara was the founder of this school. His principle was a combination of Socraticism with Eleaticism. Virtue is knowledge, but knowledge of what? It is here that the Eleatic influence became visible. With Parmenides, the Megarics believed in the One Absolute Being. All multiplicity, all motion, are illusory. the world of sense has in it no true reality. Only Being is. If virtue is knowledge, therefore, it can only be the knowledge of this Being. If the essential concept of Socrates was the Good and the essential concept of Parmenides Being, Euclid now combined the two. The Good is identified with Being. Being, the One, God, the Good, divinity, are merely different names for one and the same thing. Becoming, the many, Evil, are the names of its opposite, not-being, Multiplicity is thus identified with evil, and both are declared illusory. Evil has no real existence. The Good alone truly is. The various virtues, as benevolence, temperance, prudence, are merely different names for the one virtue, knowledge of Being.

Zeno, the Eleatic, had shown that multiplicity and motion are not only unreal but even impossible, since they are self-contradictory. The Megarics appropriated this idea, together with the dialectic of Zeno, and concluded that since not-being is impossible, Being includes all possibility. Whatever is possible is also actual. There is no such thing as a possible something, which yet does not exist.

As the Cynics found virtue in renunciation and negative independence, the Cyrenaics in the hedonistic pursuit of pleasure, so the Megarics find it in the life of philosophic contemplation, the knowledge of Being.

CHAPTER XII
PLATO

None of the predecessors of Plato had constructed a system of philosophy. What they had produced, and in great abundance, were isolated philosophical ideas, theories, hints, and suggestions. Plato was the first person in the history of the world to produce a great all-embracing system of philosophy, which has its ramifications in all departments of thought and reality. In doing this, Plato laid all previous thought under contribution. He gathered the entire harvest of Greek philosophy. All that was best in the Pythagoreans, the Eleatics, Heracleitus, and Socrates, reappears, transfigured in the system of Plato. But it is not to be imagined, on this account, that Plato was a mere eclectic, or a plagiarist, who took the best thoughts of others, and worked them into some sort of a patch-work philosophy of his own. He was, on the contrary, in the highest degree an original thinker. But like all great systems of thought, that of Plato grows out of the thought of previous thinkers. He does indeed appropriate the ideas of Heracleitus, Parmenides, and Socrates. But he does not leave them as he finds them. He takes them as the germs of a new development. They are the foundations, below ground, upon which he builds the palace of philosophy. In his hands, all previous thought becomes transfigured under the light of a new and original principle.

1. Life and Writings.

The exact date of the birth of Plato is a matter of doubt. But the date usually given, 429-7 B.C. cannot be far wrong. He came of an aristocratic Athenian family, and was possessed of sufficient wealth to enable him to command that leisure which was essential for a life devoted to philosophy. His youth coincided with the most disastrous period of Athenian history. After a bitter struggle, which lasted over a quarter of a century, the Peloponnesian war ended in the complete downfall of Athens as a political power. And the internal affairs of the State were in no less confusion than the external. Here, as elsewhere, a triumphant democracy had developed into mob-rule. Then at the close of the Peloponnesian war, the aristocratic party again came into power with the Thirty Tyrants, among whom were some of

Plato's own relatives. But the aristocratic party, so far from improving affairs, plunged at once into a reign of bloodshed, terror, and oppression. These facts have an important bearing upon the history of Plato's life. If he ever possessed any desire to adopt a political career, the actual condition of Athenian affairs must have quenched it. An aristocrat, both in thought and by birth, he could not accommodate himself to the rule of the mob. And if he ever imagined that the return of the aristocracy to power would improve matters, he must have been bitterly disillusioned by the proceedings of the Thirty Tyrants. Disgusted alike with the democracy and the aristocracy he seems to have retired into seclusion. He never once, throughout his long life, appeared as a speaker in the popular assembly. He regarded the Athenian constitution as past help.

Not much is known of the philosopher's youth. He composed poems. He was given the best education that an Athenian citizen of those days could obtain. His teacher, Cratylus, was a follower of Heracleitus, and Plato no doubt learned from him the doctrines of that philosopher. It is improbable that he allowed himself to remain unacquainted with the disputations of the Sophists, many of whom were his own contemporaries. He probably read the book of Anaxagoras, which was easily obtainable in Athens at the time. But on all these points we have no certain information. What we do know is that the decisive event in his youth, and indeed in his life, was his association with Socrates.

For the last eight years of the life of Socrates, Plato was his friend and his faithful disciple. The teaching and personality of the master constituted the supreme intellectual impulse of his life, and the inspiration of his entire thought. And the devotion and esteem which he felt for Socrates, so far from waning as the years went by, seem, on the contrary, to have grown continually stronger. For it is precisely in the latest dialogues of his long life that some of the most charming and admiring portraits of Socrates are to be found. Socrates became for him the pattern and exemplar of the true philosopher.

After the death of Socrates a second period opens in the life of Plato, the period of his travels. He migrated first to Megara, where his friend and fellow-disciple Euclid was then founding the Megaric school. The Megaric philosophy was a combination of the thought of Socrates with that of the Eleatics. And it was no doubt here, at Megara, under the influence of Euclid, that Plato formed his deeper acquaintance with the teaching of Parmenides, which exercised an all-important influence upon his own philosophy. From Megara he travelled to Cyrene, Egypt, Italy, and Sicily. In Italy he came in contact with the Pythagoreans. And to the effects of this journey may be attributed the strong Pythagorean elements which permeate his thought.

In Sicily he attended the court of Dionysius the Elder, tyrant of Syracuse. But here his conduct seems to have given grave offence. Dionysius was so angered by his moralizings and philosophical diatribes that he put Plato up to auction in the slave market. Plato narrowly escaped the fate of slavery, but was ransomed by Anniceris, the Cyrenaic. He then returned to Athens, his travels having occupied a period of about ten years.

With the return of Plato to Athens we enter upon the third and last period of his life. With the exception of two journeys to be mentioned shortly, he never again left Athens. He now appeared for the first time as a professional teacher and philosopher. He chose for the scene of his activities a gymnasium, called the Academy. Here he gradually collected round him a circle of pupils and disciples. For the rest of his life, a period of about forty years, he occupied himself in literary activity, and in the management of the school which he had founded. His manner of life was in strong contrast to that of Socrates. Only in one respect did he resemble his master. He took no fees for his teaching. Otherwise the lives of the two great men bear no resemblance to each other. Socrates had gone out into the highways and byways in search of wisdom. He had wrangled in the market-place with all comers. Plato withdrew himself into the seclusion of a school, protected from the hubbub of the world by a ring of faithful disciples. It was not to be expected that a man of Plato's refinement, culture, and aristocratic feelings, should appreciate, as Socrates, the man of the people, had done, the rough-and-tumble life of the Athenian market-place. Nor was it desirable for the advancement of philosophy that it should be so. The Socratic philosophy had suffered from the Socratic manner of life. It was unmethodical and inchoate. Systematic thought is not born of disputes at the street corner. For the development of a great world-system, such as that of Plato, laborious study and quiet seclusion were essential.

This period of Plato's mastership was broken only by two journeys to Sicily, both undertaken with political objects. Plato knew well that the perfect State, as depicted in his "Republic," was not capable of realization in the Greece of his own time. Nevertheless, he took his political philosophy very seriously. Though the perfect republic was an unattainable ideal, yet, he thought, any real reform of the State must at least proceed in the direction of that ideal. One of the essential principles of the "Republic" was that the rulers must also be philosophers. Not till philosopher and ruler were combined in one and the same person could the State be governed upon true principles. Now, in the year 368 B.C., Dionysius the Elder died, and Dionysius the younger became tyrant of Syracuse. Dionysius despatched an invitation to Plato to attend his court and give him the benefit of his advice. Here was an opportunity to experiment. Plato could train and educate a philosopher-king. He accepted the invitation. But the expedition ended disastrously. Dionysius received him with enthusiasm, and interested himself in the philosophical discourses of his teacher. But he was young, impetuous, hot-headed, and without genuine philosophic bent. His first interest gave place to weariness and irritation. Plato left Syracuse a disappointed man; and returned to Athens. Nevertheless, after the lapse of a few years, Dionysius again invited him to Syracuse, and again he accepted the invitation. But the second journey ended in disaster like the first, and Plato was even in danger of his life, but was rescued by the intervention of the Pythagoreans. He returned to Athens in his seventieth year, and lived till his death in the seclusion of his school, never again attempting to intervene in practical politics.

For more than another decade he dwelt and taught in Athens. His life was serene, quiet, and happy. He died peacefully at the age of eighty-two.

Plato's writings take the form of dialogues. In the majority of these, the chief part is taken by Socrates, into whose mouth Plato puts the exposition of his own philosophy. In a few, as for example the "Parmenides," other speakers enunciate the Platonic teaching, but even in these Socrates always plays an important rôle. Plato was not only a philosopher, but a consummate literary artist. The dialogues are genuinely dramatic, enlivened by incident, humour, and life-like characterization. Not only is the portrait of Socrates drawn with loving affection, but even the minor characters are flesh and blood.

A most important element of Plato's style is his use of myths. He does not always explain his meaning in the form of direct scientific exposition. He frequently teaches by allegories, fables, and stories, all of which may be included under the one general appellation of Platonic myths. These are often of great literary beauty, but in spite of this they involve grave disadvantages. Plato slips so easily from scientific exposition into myth, that it is often no easy matter to decide whether his statements are meant literally or allegorically. Moreover, the myths usually signify a defect in his thought itself. The fact is that the combination of poet and philosopher in one man is an exceedingly dangerous combination. I have explained before that the object of philosophy is, not merely to feel the truth, as the poet and mystic feel it, but intellectually to comprehend it, not merely to give us a series of pictures and metaphors, but a reasoned explanation of things upon scientific principles. When a man, who is at once a poet and a philosopher, cannot rationally explain a thing, it is a terrible temptation to him to substitute poetic metaphors for the explanation which is lacking. We saw, for example, that the writers of the Upanishads, who believed that the whole world issues forth from the one, absolute, imperishable, being, which they called Brahman, being unable to explain why the One thus differentiates itself into the many, took refuge in metaphors. As the sparks from the substantial fire, so, they say, do all finite beings issue forth from the One. But this explains nothing, and the aim of the philosopher is not thus vaguely to feel, but rationally to understand. Now this is not merely my view of the functions of philosophy. It is emphatically Plato's own view. In fact Plato was the originator of it. He is perpetually insisting that nothing save full rational comprehension deserves the names of knowledge and philosophy. No writer has ever used such contemptuous language as Plato used of the mere mystic and poet, who says wise and beautiful things, without in the least understanding why they are wise and beautiful. No man has formed such a low estimate of the functions of the poet and mystic. Plato is, in theory at least, the prince of rationalists and intellectualists. In practice, however, he must be convicted of the very fault he so severely censured in others. This, in fact, is the explanation of most of the Platonic myths. Wherever Plato is unable to explain anything, he covers up the gap in his system with a myth. This is particularly noticeable, for example, in the "Timaeus." Plato having, in other dialogues, developed his theory of the nature of the ultimate reality, arrives, in the "Timaeus," at the problem how the actual world is to be explained from that ultimate reality. At this point, as we shall see, Plato's system breaks down. His account of the absolute reality is defective, and in consequence, it affords no principle whereby the actual universe can be explained. In the "Timaeus," therefore, instead of a reasoned explanation, he gives us a series of wholly fanciful myths about the origin of the world. Wherever we find myths in Plato's dialogues, we may suspect that we have arrived at one of the weak points of the system.

If we are to study Plato intelligently, it is essential that we should cease to regard the dialogues as if they were all produced en bloc from a single phase of their author's mind. His literary activity extended over a period of not less than fifty years. During that time, he did not stand still. His thought, and his mode of expression, were constantly developing. If we are to understand Plato, we must obtain some clue to enable us to trace this development. And this means that we must know something of the order in which the dialogues were written. Unfortunately, however, they have not come down to us dated and numbered. It is a matter of scholarship and criticism to deduce the period at which any dialogue was written from internal evidences. Many minor points are still undecided, as well as a few questions of importance, such as the date of the "Phaedrus," which some critics place quite early and some very late in Plato's life. Neglecting these points, however, we may say in general that unanimity has been reached, and that we now know enough to be able to trace the main lines of development.

The dialogues fall into three main groups, which correspond roughly to the three periods of Plato's life. Those of the earliest group were written about the time of the death of Socrates, and before the author's journey to Megara. Some of them may have been written before the death of Socrates. This group includes the "Hippias Minor," the "Lysis," the "Charmides," the "Laches," the "Euthyphro," the "Apology," the "Crito," and the "Protagoras." The "Protagoras" is the longest, the most complex in thought, and the most developed. It is probably the latest, and forms the bridge to the second group.

All these early dialogues are short and simple, and are still, as regards their thought, entirely under the influence of Socrates. Plato has not as yet developed any philosophy of his own. He propounds the philosophy of Socrates almost unaltered. Even so, however, he is no mere plagiarist. There are throughout these dialogues evidences of freshness and originality, but these qualities exhibit themselves rather in the literary form than in the philosophical substance. We find here all the familiar Socratic propositions, that virtue is knowledge, is one, is teachable; that all men seek the good, but that men differ as to what the good is; that a man who does wrong deliberately is better than a man who does it unintentionally; and so on. Moreover, just as Socrates had occupied himself in attempting to fix the concepts of the virtues, asking "what is prudence?", "what is temperance?", and the like, so in many of these dialogues Plato pursues similar inquiries. The "Lysis" discusses the concept of friendship, the "Charmides" of temperance, the "Laches" of bravery. On the whole, the philosophical substance of these early writings is thin and meagre. There is a preponderance of incident and much biographical detail regarding Socrates. There is more art than matter. Consequently, from a purely literary point of view, these are among the most charming of Plato's dialogues, and many of them, such as the "Apology" and the "Crito," are especially popular with those who care for Plato rather as an artist than as a philosopher.

The second group of dialogues is generally connected with the period of Plato's travels. In addition to the influence of Socrates, we have now the influence of the Eleatics, which naturally connects these dialogues with the period of the philosopher's sojourn at Megara. But it is in these dialogues, too, that Plato for the first time develops his own special philosophical thesis. This is in fact his great constructive period. The central and governing principle of his philosophy is the theory of Ideas. All else hinges on this, and is dominated by this. In a sense, his whole philosophy is nothing but the theory of Ideas and what depends upon it. It is in this second period that the theory of Ideas is founded and developed, and its relationship to the Eleatic philosophy of Being discussed. We have here the spectacle of Plato's most original thoughts in the pangs of childbirth. He is now at grips with the central problems of philosophy. He is intent upon the thought itself, and cares little for the ornaments of style. He is struggling to find expression for ideas newly-formed in his mind, of which he is not yet completely master, and which he cannot manipulate with ease. Consequently, the literary graces of the first period recede into the background. There is little incident, and no humour. There is nothing but close reasoning, hard and laborious discussion.

The twin dialogues, "Gorgias" and "Theaetetus" are probably the earliest of this group. They result in nothing very definite, and are chiefly negative in character. Plato is here engaged merely in a preparatory clearing of the ground. The "Gorgias" discusses and refutes the Sophistic identification of virtue and pleasure, and attempts to show, as against it, that the good must be something objectively existent, and independent of the pleasure of the individual. The "Theaetetus," similarly, shows that truth is not, as the Sophists thought, merely the subjective impression of the individual, but is something objectively true in itself. The other dialogues of the group are the "Sophist," the "Statesman," and the "Parmenides." The "Sophist" discusses Being and not-being, and their relationship to the theory of Ideas. The "Parmenides" inquires whether the absolute reality is to be regarded, in the manner of the Eleatics, as an abstract One. It gives us, therefore, Plato's conception of the relation of his own philosophy to Eleaticism.

The dialogues of the third group are the work of Plato's maturity. He has now completely mastered his thought, and turns it with ease in all directions. Hence the style returns to the lucidity and purity of the first period. If the first period was marked chiefly by literary grace, the second by depth of thought, the third period combines both. The perfect substance is now moulded in the perfect form. But a peculiarity of all the dialogues of this period is that they take it for granted that the theory of Ideas is already established and familiar to the reader. They proceed to apply it to all departments of thought. The second period was concerned with the formulation and proof of the theory of Ideas, the third period undertakes its systematic application. Thus the "Symposium," which has for its subject the metaphysic of love, attempts to connect man's feeling for beauty with the intellectual knowledge of the Ideas. The "Philebus" applies the theory of Ideas to the sphere of ethics, the "Timaeus" to the sphere of physics, and the "Republic" to the sphere of politics. The "Phaedo" founds the doctrine of the immortality of the soul upon the theory of Ideas. The "Phaedrus" is probably to be grouped with the "Symposium." The beauty, grace, and lucidity of the style, and the fact that it assumes throughout that the theory of Ideas is a thing established, lead us to the belief that it belongs to the period of Plato's maturity. Zeller's theory that it was written at the beginning of the second period, and is then offered to the reader as a sort of sweetmeat to induce him to enter upon the laborious task of reading the "Sophist," the "Statesman," and the "Parmenides," seems to be far-fetched and unnecessary.

If the second is the great constructive period of Plato's life, the third may be described as his systematic and synthetic period. Every part of his philosophy is here linked up with every other part. All the details of the system are seen to flow from the one central principle of his thought, the theory of Ideas. Every sphere of knowledge and being is in turn exhibited in the light of that principle, is permeated and penetrated by it.

The plan for expounding Plato which first suggests itself is to go through the dialogues, one by one, and extract the doctrine of each successively. But this suggestion has to be given up as soon as it is mentioned. For although the philosophy of Plato is in itself a systematic and coherent body of thought, he did not express it in a systematic way. On the contrary, he scatters his ideas in all directions. He throws them out at random in any order. What logically comes first often appears last. It may be found at the end of a dialogue, and the next step in reasoning may make its appearance at the beginning, or even in a totally different dialogue. If, therefore, we are to get any connected view of the system, we must abandon Plato's own order of exposition, and piece the thought together for ourselves. We must begin with what logically comes first, wherever we may find it, and proceed with the exposition in the same manner.

A similar difficulty attends the question of the division of Plato's philosophy. He himself has given us no single and certain principle of division. But the principle usually adopted divides his philosophy into Dialectic, Physics, and Ethics. Dialectic, or the theory of Ideas, is Plato's doctrine of the nature of the absolute reality. Physics is the theory of phenomenal existence in space and time, and includes therefore the doctrine of the soul and its migrations, since these are happenings in time. Ethics includes politics, the theory of the duty of man as a citizen, as well as the ethics of the individual. Certain portions of the system, the doctrine of Eros, for example, do not fall very naturally into any of these divisions. But, on the other hand, though some dialogues are mixed as to their subject matter, others, and those the most important, fall almost exclusively into one or other division. For example, the "Timaeus," the "Phaedo," and the "Phaedrus," are physical. The "Philebus," the "Gorgias," and the "Republic," are ethical. The "Theaetetus," the "Sophist," and the "Parmenides," are dialectical.

2. The Theory of Knowledge.

The theory of Ideas is itself based upon the theory of knowledge. What is knowledge? What is truth? Plato opens the discussion by telling us first what knowledge and truth are not. His object here is the refutation of false theories. These must be disposed of to clear the ground preparatory to positive exposition. The first such false theory which he attacks is that knowledge is perception. To refute this is the main object of the "Theaetetus." His arguments may be summarized as follows:--

(1) That knowledge is perception is the theory of Protagoras and the Sophists, and we have seen to what results it leads. What it amounts to is that what appears to each individual true is true for that individual. But this is at any rate false in its application to our judgment of future events. The frequent mistakes which men make about the future show this. It may appear to me that I shall be Chief Justice next year. But instead of that, I find myself, perhaps, in prison. In general, what appears to each individual to be the truth about the future frequently does not turn out so in the event.

(2) Perception yields contradictory impressions. The same object appears large when near, small when removed to a distance. Compared with some things it is light, with others heavy. In one light it is white, in another green, and in the dark it has no colour at all. Looked at from one angle this piece of paper seems square, from another it appears to be a rhombus. Which of all these impressions is true? To know which is true, we must be able to exercise a choice among these varying impressions, to prefer one to another, to discriminate, to accept this and reject that. But if knowledge is perception, then we have no right to give one perception preference over another. For all perceptions are knowledge. All are true.

(3) This doctrine renders all teaching, all discussion, proof, or disproof, impossible. Since all perceptions are equally true, the child's perceptions must be just as much the truth as those of his teachers. His teachers, therefore, can teach him nothing. As to discussion and proof, the very fact that two people dispute about anything implies that they believe in the existence of an objective truth. Their impressions, if they contradict each other, cannot both be true. For if so, there is nothing to dispute about. Thus all proof and refutation are rendered futile by the theory of Protagoras.

(4) If perception is truth, man is the measure of all things, in his character as a percipient being. But since animals are also percipient beings, the lowest brute must be, equally with man, the measure of all things.

(5) The theory of Protagoras contradicts itself. For Protagoras admits that what appears to me true is true. If, therefore, it appears to me true that the doctrine of Protagoras is false, Protagoras himself must admit that it is false.

(6) It destroys the objectivity of truth, and renders the distinction between truth and falsehood wholly meaningless. The same thing is true and false at the same time, true for you and false for me. Hence it makes no difference at all whether we say that a proposition is true, or whether we say that it is false. Both statements mean the same thing, that is to say, neither of them means anything. To say that whatever I perceive is true for me merely gives a new name to my perception, but does not add any value to it.

(7) In all perception there are elements which are not contributed by the senses. Suppose I say, "This piece of paper is white." This, we might think, is a pure judgment of perception. Nothing is stated except what I perceive by means of my senses. But on consideration it turns out that this is not correct. First of all I must think "this piece of paper." Why do I call it paper? My doing so means that I have classified it. I have mentally compared it with other pieces of paper, and decided that it is of a class with them. My thought, then, involves comparison and classification. The object is a compound sensation of whiteness, squareness, etc. I can only recognise it as a piece of paper by identifying these sensations, which I have now, with sensations received from other similar objects in the past. And not only must I recognize the sameness of the sensations, but I must recognize their difference from other sensations. I must not confound the sensations I receive from paper with those which I receive from a piece of wood. Both identities and differences of sensations must be known before I can say "this piece of paper." The same is true when I go on to say that it "is white." This is only possible by classifying it with other white objects, and differentiating it from objects of other colours. But the senses themselves cannot perform these acts of comparison and contrast. Each sensation is, so to speak, an isolated dot. It cannot go beyond itself to compare itself with others. This operation must be performed by my mind, which acts as a co-

ordinating central authority, receiving the isolated sensations, combining, comparing, and contrasting them. This is particularly noticeable in cases where we compare sensations of one sense with those of another. Feeling a ball with my fingers, I say it feels round. Looking at it with my eyes, I say it looks round. But the feel is quite a different sensation from the look. Yet I use the same word, "round," to describe both. And this shows that I have identified the two sensations. This cannot be done by the senses themselves. For my eyes cannot feel, and my fingers cannot see. It must be the mind itself, standing above the senses, which performs the identification. Thus the ideas of identity and difference are not yielded to me by my senses. The intellect itself introduces them into things. Yet they are involved in all knowledge, for they are involved even in the simplest acts of knowledge, such as the proposition, "This is white." Knowledge, therefore, cannot consist simply of sense-impressions, as Protagoras thought, for even the simplest propositions contain more than sensation.

If knowledge is not the same as perception, neither is it, on the other hand, the same as opinion. That knowledge is opinion is the second false theory that Plato seeks to refute. Wrong opinion is clearly not knowledge. But even right opinion cannot be called knowledge. If I say, without any grounds for the statement, that there will be a thunderstorm next Easter Sunday, it may chance that my statement turns out to be correct. But it cannot be said that, in making this blind guess, I had any knowledge, although, as it turned out, I had right opinion. Right opinion may also be grounded, not on mere guess-work, but on something which, though better, is still not true understanding. We often feel intuitively, or instinctively, that something is true, though we cannot give any definite grounds for our belief. The belief may be quite correct, but it is not, according to Plato, knowledge. It is only right opinion. To possess knowledge, one must not only know that a thing is so, but why it is so. One must know the reasons. Knowledge must be full and complete understanding, rational comprehension, and not mere instinctive belief. It must be grounded on reason, and not on faith. Right opinion may be produced by persuasion and sophistry, by the arts of the orator and rhetorician. Knowledge can only be produced by reason. Right opinion may equally be removed by the false arts of rhetoric, and is therefore unstable and uncertain. But true knowledge cannot be thus shaken. He who truly knows and understands cannot be robbed of his knowledge by the glamour of words. Opinion, lastly, may be true or false. Knowledge can only be true.

These false theories being refuted, we can now pass to the positive side of the theory of knowledge. If knowledge is neither perception nor opinion, what is it? Plato adopts, without alteration, the Socratic doctrine that all knowledge is knowledge through concepts. This, as I explained in the lecture on Socrates, gets rid of the objectionable results of the Sophistic identification of knowledge with perception. A concept, being the same thing as a definition, is something fixed and permanent, not liable to mutation according to the subjective impressions of the individual. It gives us objective truth. This also agrees with Plato's view of opinion. Knowledge is not opinion, founded on instinct or intuition. Knowledge is founded on reason. This is the same as saying that it is founded upon concepts, since reason is the faculty of concepts.

But if Plato, in answering the question, "What is knowledge?" follows implicitly the teaching of Socrates, he yet builds upon this teaching a new and wholly un-Socratic metaphysic of his own. The Socratic theory of knowledge he now converts into a theory of the nature of reality. This is the subject-matter of Dialectic.

3. Dialectic, or the Theory of Ideas.

The concept had been for Socrates merely a rule of thought. Definitions, like guide-rails, keep thought upon the straight path; we compare any act with the definition of virtue in order to ascertain whether it is virtuous. But what was for Socrates merely regulative of thought, Plato now transforms into a metaphysical substance. His theory of Ideas is the theory of the objectivity of concepts. That the concept is not merely an idea in the mind, but something which has a reality of its own, outside and independent of the mind--this is the essence of the philosophy of Plato.

How did Plato arrive at this doctrine? It is founded upon the view that truth means the correspondence of one's ideas with the facts of existence. If I see a lake of water, and if there really is such a lake, then my idea is true. But if there is no lake, then my idea is false. It is an hallucination. Truth, according to this view, means that the thought in my mind is a copy of something outside my mind. Falsehood consists in having an idea which is not a copy of anything which really exists. Knowledge, of course, means knowledge of the truth. And when I say that a thought in my mind is knowledge, I must therefore mean that this thought is a copy of something that exists. But we have already seen that knowledge is the knowledge of concepts. And if a concept is true knowledge, it can only be true in virtue of the fact that it corresponds to an objective reality. There must, therefore, be general ideas or concepts, outside my mind. It were a contradiction to suppose, on the one hand, that the concept is true knowledge, and on the other, that it corresponds to nothing external to us. This would be like saying that my idea of the lake of water is a true idea, but that no such lake really exists. The concept in my mind must be a copy of the concept outside it.

Now if knowledge by concepts is true, our experiences through sensation must be false. Our senses make us aware of many individual horses. Our intellect gives us the concept of the horse in general. If the latter is the sole truth, the former must be false. And this can only mean that the objects of sensation have no true reality. What has reality is the concept; what has no reality is the individual thing which is perceived by the senses. This and that particular horse have no true being. Reality belongs only to the idea of the horse in general.

Let us approach this theory from a somewhat different direction. Suppose I ask you the question, "What is beauty?" You point to a rose, and say, "Here is beauty." And you say the same of a woman's face, a piece of woodland scenery, and a clear moonlight night. But I answer that this is not what I want to know. I did not ask what things are beautiful, but what is beauty. I did not ask for many things, but for one thing, namely, beauty. If beauty is a rose, it cannot be moonlight, because a rose and moonlight are quite different things. By beauty we mean, not many things, but one. This is proved by the fact that we use only one word for it. And what I want to know is what this one beauty is, which is distinct from all beautiful objects. Perhaps you will say that there is no such thing as beauty apart from beautiful objects, and that, though we use one word, yet this is only a manner of speech, and that there are in reality many beauties, each residing in a beautiful object. In that case, I observe that, though the many beauties are all different, yet, since you use the one word to describe them all, you evidently think that they are similar to each other. How do you know that they are similar? Your eyes cannot inform you of this similarity, because it involves comparison, and we have already seen that comparison is an act of the mind, and not of the senses. You must therefore have an idea of beauty in your mind, with which you compare the various beautiful objects and so recognise them as all resembling your idea of beauty, and therefore as resembling each other. So that there is at any rate an idea of one beauty in your mind. Either this idea corresponds to something outside you, or it does not. In the latter case, your idea of beauty is a mere invention, a figment of your own brain. If so, then, in judging external objects by your subjective idea, and in making it the standard of whether they are beautiful or not, you are back again at the position of the Sophists. You are making yourself and the fancies of your individual brain the standard of external truth. Therefore, the only alternative is to believe that there is not only an idea of beauty in your mind, but that there is such a thing as the one beauty itself, of which your idea is a copy. This beauty exists outside the mind, and it is something distinct from all beautiful objects.

What has been said of beauty may equally be said of justice, or of goodness, or of whiteness, or of heaviness. There are many just acts, but only one justice, since we use one word for it. This justice must be a real thing, distinct from all particular just acts. Our ideas of justice are copies of it. So also there are many white objects, but also the one whiteness.

Of the above examples, several are very exalted moral ideas, such as beauty, justice, and goodness. But the case of whiteness will serve to show that the theory attributes reality not only to exalted ideas, but to others also. In fact, we might quite well substitute evil for goodness, and all the same arguments would apply. Or we might take a corporeal object such as the horse, and ask what "horse" means. It does not mean the many individual horses, for since one word is used it must mean one thing, which is related to individual horses, just as whiteness is related to individual white things. It means the universal horse, the idea of the horse in general, and this, just as much as goodness or beauty, must be something objectively real.

Now beauty, justice, goodness, whiteness, the horse in general, are all concepts. The idea of beauty is formed by including what is common to all beautiful objects, and excluding those points in which they differ. And this, as we have seen, is just what is meant by a concept. Plato's theory, therefore, is that concepts are objective realities. And he gives to these objective concepts the technical name Ideas. This is his answer to the chief question of philosophy, namely, what, amid all the appearances and unrealities of things, is that absolute and ultimate reality, from which all else is to be explained? It consists, for Plato, in Ideas.

Let us see next what the characteristics of the Ideas are. In the first place, they are substances. Substance is a technical term in philosophy, but its philosophical meaning is merely a more consistent development of its popular meaning. In common talk, we generally apply the word substance to material things such as iron, brass, wood, or water. And we say that these substances possess qualities. For example, hardness and shininess are qualities of the substance iron. The qualities cannot exist apart from the substances. They do not exist on their own account, but are dependent on the substance. The shininess cannot exist by itself. There must be a shiny something. But, according to popular ideas, though the qualities are not independent of the substance, the substance is independent of the qualities. The qualities derive their reality from the substance. But the substance has reality in itself. The philosophical use of the term substance is simply a more consistent application of this idea. Substance means, for the philosopher, that which has its whole being in itself, whose reality does not flow into it from anything else, but which is the source of its own reality. It is self-caused, and self-determined. It is the ground of other things, but itself has no ground except itself. For example, if we believe the popular Christian idea that God created the world, but is Himself an ultimate and uncreated being, then, since the world depends for its existence upon God, but God's existence depends only upon Himself, God is a substance and the world is not. In this sense the word is correctly used in the Creed where it speaks of God as "three persons, but one substance." Again, if, with the Idealists, we think that mind is a self-existent reality, and that matter owes its existence to mind, then in that case matter is not substance, but mind is. In this technical sense the Ideas are substances. They are absolute and ultimate realities. Their whole being is in themselves. They depend on nothing, but all things depend on them. They are the first principles of the universe.

Secondly, the Ideas are universal. An Idea is not any particular thing. The Idea of the horse is not this or that horse. It is the general concept of all horses. It is the universal horse. For this reason the Ideas are, in modern times, often called "universals."

Thirdly, the Ideas are not things, but thoughts. There is no such thing as the horse-in-general. If there were, we should be able to find it somewhere, and it would then be a particular thing instead of a universal. But in saying that the Ideas are thoughts, there are two mistakes to be carefully avoided. The first is to suppose that they are the thoughts of a person, that they are your thoughts or my thoughts. The second is to suppose that they are thoughts in the mind of God. Both these views are wrong. It would be absurd to suppose that our thoughts can be the cause of the universe. Our concepts are indeed copies of the Ideas, but to confuse them with the Ideas themselves is, for Plato, as absurd as to confuse our idea of a mountain with the mountain itself. Nor are they the thoughts of God. They are indeed sometimes spoken of as the "Ideas in the divine mind." But this is only a figurative expression. We can, if we like, talk of the sum of all the Ideas as constituting the "divine mind." But this means nothing in particular, and is only a poetical phrase. Both these mistakes are due to the fact that we find it difficult to conceive of thoughts without a thinker. This, however, is just what Plato meant. They are not subjective ideas, that is, the ideas in a particular and existent mind. They are objective Ideas, thoughts which have reality on their own account, independently of any mind.

Fourthly, each Idea is a unity. It is the one amid the many. The Idea of man is one, although individual men are many. There cannot be more than one Idea for each class of objects. If there were several Ideas of justice, we should have to seek for the common element among them, and this common element would itself constitute the one Idea of justice.

Fifthly, the Ideas are immutable and imperishable. A concept is the same as a definition. And the whole point in a definition is that it should always be the same. The object of a definition is to compare individual things with it, and to see whether they agree with it or not. But if the definition of a triangle differed from day to day, it would be useless, since we could never say whether any particular figure were a triangle or not, just as the standard yard in the Tower of London would be useless if it changed in length, and were twice as long to-day as it was yesterday. A definition is thus something absolutely permanent, and a definition is only the expression in words of the nature of an Idea. Consequently the Ideas cannot change. The many beautiful objects arise and pass away, but the one Beauty neither begins nor ends. It is eternal, unchangeable, and imperishable. The many beautiful things are but the fleeting expressions of the one eternal beauty. The definition of man would remain the same, even if all men were destroyed. The Idea of man is eternal, and remains untouched by the birth, old age, decay, and death, of individual men.

Sixthly, the Ideas are the Essences of all things. The definition gives us what is essential to a thing. If we define man as a rational animal, this means that reason is of the essence of man. The fact that this man has a turned-up nose, and that man red hair, are accidental facts, not essential to their humanity. We do not include them in the definition of man.

Seventhly, each Idea is, in its own kind, an absolute perfection, and its perfection is the same as its reality. The perfect man is the one universal type-man, that is, the Idea of man, and all individual men deviate more or less from this perfect type. In so far as they fall short of it, they are imperfect and unreal.

Eighthly, the Ideas are outside space and time. That they are outside space is obvious. If they were in space, they would have to be in some particular place. We ought to be able to find them somewhere. A telescope or microscope might reveal them. And this would mean that they are individual and particular things, and not universals at all. They are also outside time. For they are unchangeable and eternal; and this does not mean that they are the same at all times. If that were so, their immutability would be a matter of experience, and not of reason. We should, so to speak, have to look at them from time to time to see that they had not really changed. But their immutability is not a matter of experience, but is known to thought. It is not merely that they are always the same in time, but that time is irrelevant to them. They are timeless. In the "Timaeus" eternity is distinguished from infinite time. The latter is described as a mere copy of eternity.

Ninthly, the Ideas are rational, that is to say, they are apprehended through reason. The finding of the common element in the manifold is the work of inductive reason, and through this alone is knowledge of the Ideas possible. This should be noted by those persons who imagine that Plato was some sort of benevolent mystic. The imperishable One, the absolute reality, is apprehended, not by intuition, or in any kind of mystic ecstasy, but only by rational cognition and laborious thought.

Lastly, towards the end of his life, Plato identified the Ideas with the Pythagorean numbers. We know this from Aristotle, but it is not mentioned in the dialogues of Plato himself. It appears to have been a theory adopted in old age, and set forth in the lectures which Aristotle attended. It is a retrograde step, and tends to degrade the great and lucid idealism of Plato into a mathematical mysticism. In this, as in other respects, the influence of the Pythagoreans upon Plato was harmful.

It results from this whole theory of Ideas that there are two sources of human experience, sense-perception and reason. Sense-perception has for its object the world of sense; reason has for its object the Ideas. The world of sense has all the opposite characteristics to the Ideas. The Ideas are absolute reality, absolute Being. Objects of sense are absolute unreality, not-being, except in so far as the Ideas are in them. Whatever reality they have they owe to the Ideas. There is in Plato's system a principle of absolute not-being which we shall consider when we come to deal with his Physics. Objects of sense participate both in the Ideas and in this not-being. They are, therefore, half way between Being and not-being. They are half real. Ideas, again, are universal; things of sense are always particular and individual. The Idea is one, the sense-object is always a multiplicity. Ideas are outside space and time, things of sense are both temporal and spatial. The Idea is eternal and immutable; sense-objects are changeable and in perpetual flux.

As regards the last point, Plato adopts the view of Heracleitus that there is an absolute Becoming, and he identifies it with the world of sense, which contains nothing stable and permanent, but is a constant flow. The Idea always is, and never becomes; the thing of sense always becomes, and never is. It is for this reason that, in the opinion of Plato, no knowledge of the world of sense is possible, for one can have no knowledge of that which changes from moment to moment. Knowledge is only possible if its subject stands fixed before the mind, is permanent and changeless. The only knowledge, then, is knowledge of the Ideas.

This may seem, at first sight, a very singular doctrine. That there can be no knowledge of sense-objects would, it might seem to us moderns, involve the denial that modern physical science, with all its exactitude and accumulated knowledge, is knowledge at all. And surely, though all earthly things arise and pass away, many of them last long enough to admit of knowledge. Surely the mountains are sufficiently permanent to allow us to know something of them. They have relative, though not absolute, permanence. This criticism is partly justified. Plato did underestimate the value of physical knowledge. But for the most part, the criticism is a misunderstanding. By the world of sense Plato means bare sensation with no rational element in it. Now physical science has not such crude sensation for its object. Its objects are rationalized sensations. If, in

Plato's manner, we think only of pure sensation, then it is true that it is nothing but a constant flux without stability; and knowledge of it is impossible. The mountains are comparatively permanent. But our sensation of the mountains is perpetually changing. Every change of light, every cloud that passes over the sun, changes the colours and the shades. Every time we move from one situation to another, the mountain appears a different shape. The permanence of the mountain itself is due to the fact that all these varying sensations are identified as sensations of one and the same object. The idea of identity is involved here, and it is, as it were, a thread upon which these fleeting sensations are strung. But the idea of identity cannot be obtained from the senses. It is introduced into things by reason. Hence knowledge of this permanent mountain is only possible through the exercise of reason. In Plato's language, all we can know of the mountain is the Ideas in which it participates. To revert to a previous example, even the knowledge "this paper is white" involves the activity of intellect, and is impossible through sensation alone. Bare sensation is a flow, of which no knowledge is possible.

Aristotle observes that Plato's theory of Ideas has three sources, the teachings of the Eleatics, of Heracleitus, and of Socrates. From Heracleitus, Plato took the notion of a sphere of Becoming, and it appears in his system as the world of sense. From the Eleatics he took the idea of a sphere of absolute Being. From Socrates he took the doctrine of concepts, and proceeded to identify the Eleatic Being with the Socratic concepts. This gives him his theory of Ideas.

Sense objects, so far as they are knowable, that is so far as they are more than bare sensations, are so only because the Idea resides in them. And this yields the clue to Plato's teaching regarding the relation of sense objects to the Ideas. The Ideas are, in the first place the cause, that is to say, the ground (not the mechanical cause) of sense-objects. The Ideas are the absolute reality by which individual things must be explained. The being of things flows into them from the Ideas. They are "copies," "imitations," of the Ideas. In so far as they resemble the Idea, they are real; in so far as they differ from it, they are unreal. In general, sense objects are, in Plato's opinion, only very dim, poor and imperfect copies of the Ideas. They are mere shadows, and half-realities. Another expression frequently used by Plato to express this relationship is that of "participation." Things participate in the Ideas. White objects participate in the one whiteness, beautiful objects, in the one beauty. In this way beauty itself is the cause or explanation of beautiful objects, and so of all other Ideas. The Ideas are thus both transcendent and immanent; immanent in so far as they reside in the things of sense, transcendent inasmuch as they have a reality of their own apart from the objects of sense which participate in them. The Idea of man would still be real even if all men were destroyed, and it was real before any man existed, if there ever was such a time. For the Ideas, being timeless, cannot be real now and not then.

Of what kinds of things are there Ideas? That there are moral Ideas, such as Justice, Goodness, and Beauty, Ideas of corporeal things, such as horse, man, tree, star, river, and Ideas of qualities, such as whiteness, heaviness, sweetness, we have already seen. But there are Ideas not only of natural corporeal objects, but likewise of manufactured articles; there are Ideas of beds, tables, clothes. And there are Ideas not only of exalted moral entities, such as Beauty and Justice. There are also the Ideal Ugliness, and the Ideal Injustice. There are even Ideas of the positively nauseating, such as hair, filth, and dirt. This is asserted in the "Parmenides." In that dialogue Plato's teaching is put into the mouth of Parmenides. He questions the young Socrates whether there are Ideas of hair, filth, and dirt. Socrates denies that there can be Ideas of such base things. But Parmenides corrects him, and tells him that, when he has attained the highest philosophy, he will no longer despise such things. Moreover, these Ideas of base things are just as much perfection in their kind as Beauty and Goodness are in theirs. In general, the principle is that there must be an Idea wherever a concept can be formed; that is, wherever there is a class of many things called by one name.

We saw, in treating of the Eleatics, that for them the absolute Being contained no not-being, and the absolute One no multiplicity. And it was just because they denied all not-being and multiplicity of the absolute reality that they were unable to explain the world of existence, and were forced to deny it altogether. The same problem arises for Plato. Is Being absolutely excludent of not-being? Is the Absolute an abstract One, utterly exclusive of the many? Is his philosophy a pure monism? Is it a pluralism? Or is it a combination of the two? These questions are discussed in the "Sophist" and the "Parmenides."

Plato investigates the relations of the One and the many, Being and not-being, quite in the abstract. He decides the principles involved, and leaves it to the reader to apply them to the theory of Ideas. Whether the Absolute is one or many, Being or not-being, can be decided independently of any particular theory of the nature of the Absolute, and therefore independently of Plato's own theory, which was that the Absolute consists of Ideas. Plato does not accept the Eleatic abstraction. The One cannot be simply one, for every unity must necessarily be a multiplicity. The many and the One are correlative ideas which involve each other. Neither is thinkable without the other. A One which is not many is as absurd an abstraction as a whole which has no parts. For the One can only be defined as that which is not many, and the many can only be defined as the not-one. The One is unthinkable except as standing out against a background of the many. The idea of the One therefore involves the idea of the many, and cannot be thought without it. Moreover, an abstract One is unthinkable and unknowable, because all thought and knowledge consist in applying predicates to subjects, and all predication involves the duality of its subject.

Consider the simplest affirmation that can be made about the One, namely, "The One is." Here we have two things, "the One," and "is," that is to say, being. The proposition means that the One is Being. Hence the One is two. Firstly, it is itself, "One." Secondly, it is "Being," and the proposition affirms that these two things are one. Similarly with any other predicate we apply to the One. Whatever we say of it involves its duality. Thus we find that all systems of thought which postulate an abstract unity as ultimate reality, such as Eleaticism, Hinduism, and the system of Spinoza, attempt to avoid the difficulty by saying nothing positive about the One. They apply to it only negative predicates, which tell us not what it is, but what it is not.

Thus the Hindus speak of Brahman as formless, immutable, imperishable, unmoved, uncreated. But this, of course, is a futile expedient. In the first place, even a negative predicate involves the duality of the subject. And, in the second place, a negative predicate is always, by implication, a positive one. You cannot have a negative without a positive. To deny one thing is to affirm its opposite. To deny motion of the One, by calling it the unmoved, is to affirm rest of it. Thus a One which is not also a many is unthinkable. Similarly, the idea of the many is inconceivable without the idea of the One. For the many is many ones. Hence the One and the many cannot be separated in the Eleatic manner. Every unity must be a unity of the many. And every many is ipso facto a unity, since we think the many in one idea, and, if we did not, we should not even know that it is a many. The Absolute must therefore be neither an abstract One, nor an abstract many. It must be a many in one.

Similarly, Being cannot totally exclude not-being. They are, just as much as the One and the many, correlatives, which mutually involve each other. The being of anything is the not-being of its opposite. The being of light is the not-being of darkness. All being, therefore, has not-being in it.

Let us apply these principles to the theory of Ideas. The absolute reality, the world of Ideas, is many, since there are many Ideas, but it is one, because the Ideas are not isolated units, but members of a single organized system. There is, in fact, a hierarchy of Ideas. Just as the one Idea presides over many individual things of which it is the common element, so one higher Idea presides over many lower Ideas, and is the common element in them. And over this higher Idea, together with many others, a still higher Idea will rule. For example, the Ideas of whiteness, redness, blueness, are all subsumed under the one Idea of colour. The Ideas of sweetness and bitterness come under the one Idea of taste. But the Ideas of colour and taste themselves stand under the still higher Idea of quality. In this way, the Ideas form, as it were, a pyramid, and to this pyramid there must be an apex. There must be one highest Idea, which is supreme over all the others. This Idea will be the one final and absolutely real Being which is the ultimate ground, of itself, of the other Ideas, and of the entire universe.

This Idea is, Plato tells us, the Idea of the Good. We have seen that the world of Ideas is many, and we now see that it is one. For it is one single system culminating in one supreme Idea, which is the highest expression of its unity. Moreover, each separate Idea is, in the same way, a many in one. It is one in regard to itself. That is to say, if we ignore its relations to other Ideas, it is, in itself, single. But as it has also many relations to other Ideas, it is, in this way, a multiplicity.

Every Idea is likewise a Being which contains not-being. For each Idea combines with some Ideas and not with others. Thus the Idea of corporeal body combines both with the Idea of rest and that of motion. But the Ideas of rest and motion will not combine with each other. The Idea of rest, therefore, is Being in regard to itself, not-being in regard to the Idea of motion, for the being of rest is the not-being of motion. All Ideas are Being in regard to themselves, and not-being in regard to all those other Ideas with which they do not combine.

In this way there arises a science of Ideas which is called dialectic. This word is sometimes used as identical with the phrase, "theory of Ideas." But it is also used, in a narrower sense, to mean the science which has to do with the knowledge of which Ideas will combine and which not. Dialectic is the correct joining and disjoining of Ideas. It is the knowledge of the relations of all the Ideas to each other.

The attainment of this knowledge is, in Plato's opinion, the chief problem of philosophy. To know all the Ideas, each in itself and in its relations to other Ideas, is the supreme task. This involves two steps. The first is the formation of concepts. Its object is to know each Idea separately, and its procedure is by inductive reason to find the common element in which the many individual objects participate. The second step consists in the knowledge of the inter-relation of Ideas, and involves the two processes of classification and division. Classification and division both have for their object to arrange the lower Ideas under the proper higher Ideas, but they do this in opposite ways. One may begin with the lower Ideas, such as redness, whiteness, etc., and range them under their higher Idea, that of colour. This is classification. Or one may begin with the higher Idea, colour, and divide it into the lower Ideas, red, white, etc. Classification proceeds from below upwards. Division proceeds from above downwards. Most of the examples of division which Plato gives are divisions by dichotomy. We may either divide colour straight away into red, blue, white, etc.; or we may divide each class into two sub-classes. Thus colour will be divided into red and not-red, not-red into white and not-white, not-white into blue and not-blue, and so on. This latter process is division by dichotomy, and Plato prefers it because, though it is tedious, it is very exhaustive and systematic.

Plato's actual performance of the supreme task of dialectic, the classification and arrangement of all Ideas, is not great. He has made no attempt to complete it. All he has done is to give us numerous examples. And this is, in reality, all that can be expected, for the number of Ideas is obviously infinite, and therefore the task of arranging them cannot be completed. There is, however, one important defect in the dialectic, which Plato ought certainly to have remedied. The supreme Idea, he tells us, is the Good. This, as being the ultimate reality, is the ground of all other Ideas. Plato ought therefore to have derived all other Ideas from it, but this he has not done. He merely asserts, in a more or less dogmatic way, that the Idea of the Good is the highest, but does nothing to connect it with the other Ideas. It is easy to see, however, why he made this assertion. It is, in fact, a necessary logical outcome of his system. For every Idea is perfection in its kind. All the Ideas have perfection in common. And just as the one beauty is the Idea which presides over all beautiful things, so the one perfection must be the supreme Idea which presides over all the perfect Ideas. The supreme Idea, therefore, must be perfection itself, that is to say, the Idea of the Good. On the other hand it might, with equal force, be argued that since all the Ideas are substances, therefore the highest Idea is the Idea of substance. All that can be said is that Plato has left these matters in obscurity, and has merely asserted that the highest Idea is the Good.

Consideration of the Idea of the Good leads us naturally to enquire how far Plato's system is teleological in character. A little consideration will show that it is out and out teleological. We can see this both by studying the many lower Ideas, and the one supreme Idea. Each Idea is perfection of its kind. And each Idea is the ground of the existence of the individual objects which come under it. Thus the explanation of white objects is the perfect whiteness, of beautiful objects the perfect beauty. Or we may take as our example the Idea of the State which Plato describes in the "Republic." The ordinary view is that Plato was describing a State which was the invention of his own fancy, and is therefore to be regarded as entirely unreal. This is completely to misunderstand Plato. So far was he from thinking the ideal State unreal, that he regarded it, on the contrary, as the only real State. All existent States, such as the Athenian or the Spartan, are unreal in so far as they differ from the ideal State. And moreover, this one reality, the ideal State, is the ground of the existence of all actual States. They owe their existence to its reality. Their existence can only be explained by it. Now since the ideal State is not yet reached in fact, but is the perfect State towards which all actual States tend, it is clear that we have here a teleological principle. The real explanation of the State is not to be found in its beginnings in history, in an original contract, or in biological necessities, but in its end, the final or perfect State. Or, if we prefer to put it so; the true beginning is the end. The end must be in the beginning, potentially and ideally, otherwise it could never begin: It is the same with all other things. Man is explained by the ideal man, the perfect man; white things by the perfect whiteness, and so on. Everything is explained by its end, and not by its beginning. Things are not explained by mechanical causes, but by reasons.

And the teleology of Plato culminates in the Idea of the Good. That Idea is the final explanation of all other Ideas, and of the entire universe. And to place the final ground of all things in perfection itself means that the universe arises out of that perfect end towards which all things move.

Another matter which requires elucidation here is the place which the conception of God holds in Plato's system. He frequently uses the word God both in the singular and the plural, and seems to slip with remarkable ease from the monotheistic to the polytheistic manner of speaking. In addition to the many gods, we have frequent reference to the one supreme

Creator, controller, and ruler of the world, who is further conceived as a Being providentially watching over the lives of men. But in what relation does this supreme God stand to the Ideas, and especially to the Idea of the Good? If God is separate from the highest Idea, then, as Zeller points out, only three relations are possible, all of which are equally objectionable. Firstly, God may be the cause or ground of the Idea of the Good. But this destroys the substantiality of the Idea, and indeed, destroys Plato's whole system. The very essence of his philosophy is that the Idea is the ultimate reality, which is self-existent, and owes its being to nothing else. But this theory makes it a mere creature of God, dependent on Him for its existence. Secondly, God may owe His being to the Idea. The Idea may be the ground of God's existence as it is the ground of all else in the universe. But this theory does violence to the idea of God, turning Him into a mere derivative existence, and, in fact, into an appearance. Thirdly, God and the Idea may be co-ordinate in the system as equally primordial independent ultimate realities. But this means that Plato has given two mutually inconsistent accounts of the ultimate reality, or, if not, that his system is a hopeless dualism. As none of these theories can be maintained, it must be supposed that God is identical with the Idea of the Good, and we find certain expressions in the "Philebus" which seem clearly to assert this. But in that case God is not a personal God at all, since the Idea is not a person. The word God, if used in this way, is merely a figurative term for the Idea. And this is the most probable theory, if we reflect that there is in fact no room for a personal God in a system which places all reality in the Idea, and that to introduce such a conception threatens to break up the whole system. Plato probably found it useful to take the popular conceptions about the personality of God or the gods and use them, in mythical fashion, to express his Ideas. Those parts of Plato which speak of God, and the governance of God, are to be interpreted on the same principles as the other Platonic myths.

Before closing our discussion of dialectic, it may be well to consider what place it occupies in the life of man, and what importance is attached to it. Here Plato's answer is emphatic. Dialectic is the crown of knowledge, and knowledge is the crown of life. All other spiritual activities have value only in so far as they lead up to the knowledge of the Idea. All other subjects of intellectual study are merely preparatory to the study of philosophy. The special sciences have no value in themselves, but they have value inasmuch as their definitions and classifications form a preparation for the knowledge of Ideas. Mathematics is important because it is a stepping-stone from the world of sense to the Ideas. Its objects, namely, numbers and geometrical figures, resemble the Ideas in so far as they are immutable, and they resemble sense-objects in so far as they are in space or time. In the educational curriculum of Plato, philosophy comes last. Not everyone may study it. And none may study it till he has been through all the preparatory stages of education, which form a rigorous discipline of the mind before it finally enters upon dialectic. Thus all knowledge ends in dialectic, and that life has not attained its end which falls short of philosophy.

Perhaps the most striking illustration of the subordination of all spiritual activities to philosophy is to be found in the doctrine of Eros, or Love. The phrase "platonic love" is on the lips of many, but, as a rule, something very different from Plato's own doctrine is meant. According to him, love is always concerned with beauty, and his teaching on the subject is expounded chiefly in the "Symposium," He believed that before birth the soul dwelt disembodied in the pure contemplation of the world of Ideas. Sinking down into a body, becoming immersed in the world of sense, it forgets the Ideas. The sight of a beautiful object reminds it of that one Idea of beauty of which the object is a copy. This accounts for the mystic rapture, the emotion, the joy, with which we greet the sight of the beautiful. Since Plato had expressly declared that there are Ideas of the ugly as well as of the beautiful, that there are Ideas, for example, of hair, filth, and dirt, and since these Ideas are just as divine and perfect as the Idea of the beautiful, we ought, on this theory, to greet the ugly, the filthy, and the nauseating, with a ravishment of joy similar to that which we experience in the presence of beauty. Why this is not the case Plato omitted to explain. However, having learned to love the one beautiful object, the soul passes on to the love of others. Then it perceives that it is the same beauty which reveals itself in all these. It passes from the love of beautiful forms to the love of beautiful souls, and from that to the love of beautiful sciences. It ceases to be attached to the many objects, as such, that is to say, to the sensuous envelopes of the Idea of beauty. Love passes into the knowledge of the Idea of beauty itself, and from this to the knowledge of the world of Ideas in general. It passes in fact into philosophy.

In this development there are two points which we cannot fail to note. In the first place, emotional love is explained as being simply the blind groping of reason towards the Idea. It is reason which has not yet recognized itself as such. It appears, therefore, in the guise of feeling. Secondly, the later progress of the soul's love is simply the gradual recognition of itself by reason. When the soul perceives that the beauty in all objects is the same, that it is the common element amid the many, this is nothing but the process of inductive reasoning. And this development ends at last in the complete rational cognition of the world of Ideas, in a word, philosophy. Love is but an instinctive reason. The animal has no feeling of the beautiful, just because it has no reason. Love of the beautiful is founded upon the nature of man, not as a percipient or feeling being, but as a rational being. And it must end in the complete recognition of reason by itself, not in the feeling and intuition, but in the rational comprehension, of the Idea.

One can imagine what Plato's answer would be to the sort of vulgarians and philistines who want to know what the use of philosophy is, and in what way it is "practical." To answer such a question is for Plato impossible, because the question itself is illegitimate. For a thing to have a use involves that it is a means towards an end. Fire has use, because it may be made a means towards the cooking of food. Money is useful, because it is a means to the acquisition of goods. That which is an end in itself, and not a means towards any further end, cannot possibly have any use. To suggest that philosophy ought to have use is, therefore, to put the cart before the horse, to invert the whole scale of values. It suggests that philosophy is a means towards some further end, instead of being the absolute end to which all other things are means. Philosophy is not for anything. Everything else is for it. And, if this seems an exaggerated or unpractical view, we may at least remember that this is the view taken by the religious consciousness of man. Religion makes the supreme end of life the knowledge of, and communion with, God. God is for religion what the Idea is for philosophy. God is a figurative name for the Idea. To place the end of life in the knowledge of the Absolute, or the Idea, is therefore the teaching both of philosophy and religion.

4. Physics, or the Theory of Existence.

Dialectic is the theory of reality, physics the theory of existence, dialectic of that which lies behind things as their ground, physics of the things which are thus grounded. That is to say, physics is concerned with phenomena and appearances, things which exist in space and time, as opposed to the timeless and non-spatial Ideas. Things of this kind are both corporeal and incorporeal. Physics falls therefore into two parts, the doctrine of the outward corporeality, the world, with its incorporeal essence, the World-Soul, and the doctrine of the incorporeal soul of man.

(a) The Doctrine of the World.

If, in the dialectic, Plato has given an account of the nature of the first principle and ground of all things, the problem now arises of explaining how the actual universe of things arises out of that ground, how it is derived from the first principle. In other words, the Ideas being the absolute reality, how does the world of sense, and, in general, the existent universe, arise out of the Ideas? Faced with this problem, the system of Plato broke down. The things of sense are, we are told, "copies" or "imitations" of the Ideas. They "participate" in the Ideas. So far, so good. But why should there be any copies of the Ideas? Why should the Ideas give rise to copies of themselves, and how is the production of these copies effected? To these questions Plato has no answer, and he therefore has recourse to the use of myths. Poetic description here takes the place of scientific explanation.

This poetic description of the origin of the world is to be found in the "Timaeus." We have seen that the Ideas are absolute Being, and that things of sense are half real and half unreal. They are partly real because they participate in Being. They are partly unreal because they participate in not-being. There must be, therefore, a principle of absolute not-being. This, in Plato's opinion, is matter. Things of sense are copies of the Ideas fashioned out of, or stamped upon, matter. But Plato does not understand by matter what we, in modern times, understand by it. Matter, in our sense, is always some particular kind of matter. It is brass, or wood, or iron, or stone. It is matter which has determinate character and quality. But the possession of specific character means that it is matter with the copy of Ideas already stamped upon it. Since iron exists in great quantities in the world, and there is a common element in all the various pieces of iron, by virtue of which all are classed together, there must be a concept of iron. There is, therefore, an Idea of iron in the world of Ideas. And the iron which we find in the earth must be matter which is already formed into a copy of this Idea. It participates in the Idea of iron. The same remarks apply to any other particular kind of matter. In fact, all form, all the specific characters and features of matter, as we know it, are due to the operation of the Ideas. Hence matter as it is in itself, before the image of the Ideas is stamped upon it, must be absolutely without quality, featureless, formless. But to be absolutely without any quality is to be simply nothing at all. This matter is, therefore, as Plato says, absolute not-being. Zeller conjectures, probably rightly, that what Plato meant was simply empty space. Empty space is an existent not-being, and it is totally indeterminate and formless. It accords with this view that Plato adopted the Pythagorean tenet that the differential qualities of material substances are due to their smallest particles being regular geometrical figures limited out of the unlimited, that is, out of space. Thus earth is composed of cubes. That is to say, empty space when bound into cubes (the limiting of the unlimited) becomes earth. The smallest particles of fire are tetrahedra, of air octahedra, of water icosahedra.

We have, then, on the one hand, the world of Ideas, on the other, matter, an absolutely formless, chaotic, mass. By impressing the images of the Ideas upon this mass, "things" arise, that is to say, the specific objects of sense. They thus participate both in Being and in not-being. But how is this mixing of Being and not-being brought about? How do the Ideas come to have their images stamped upon matter? It is at this point that we enter upon the region of myth. Up to this point Plato is certainly to be taken literally. He of course believed in the reality of the world of Ideas, and he no doubt also believed in his principle of matter. And he thought that the objects of sense are to be explained as copies of the Ideas impressed upon matter. But now, with the problem how this copying is brought about, Plato leaves the method of scientific explanation behind. If the Ideas are the absolute ground of all things, then the copying process must be done by the Ideas themselves. They must themselves be made the principles for the production of things. But this is, for Plato, impossible. For production involves change. If the Ideas produce things out of themselves, the Ideas must in the process undergo change. But Plato has declared them to be absolutely unchangeable, and to be thus immutable is to be sterile. Hence the Ideas have within themselves no principle for the production of things, and the scientific explanation of things by this means becomes impossible. Hence there is nothing for it but to have recourse to myth. Plato can only imagine that things are produced by a world-former, or designer, who, like a human artist, fashions the plastic matter into images of the Ideas.

God, the Creator, the world-designer, finds beside him, on the one hand, the Ideas, on the other, formless matter. First, he creates the World-Soul. This is incorporeal, but occupies space. He spreads it out like a huge net in empty space. He bisects it, and bends the two halves into an inner and an outer circle, these circles being destined to become the spheres of the planets and the stars respectively. He takes matter and binds it into the four elements, and these elements he builds into the empty framework of the World-Soul. When this is done, the creation of the universe is complete. The rest of the "Timaeus" is occupied with the details of Plato's ideas of astronomy and physical science. These are mostly worthless and tedious, and we need not pursue them here. But we may mention that Plato, of course, regarded the earth as the centre of the world. The stars, which are divine beings, revolve around it. They necessarily move in circles, because the circle is the perfect figure. The stars, being divine, are governed solely by reason, and their movement must therefore be circular, because a circular motion is the motion of reason.

The above account of the origin of the world is merely myth, and Plato knows that it is myth. What he apparently did believe in, however, was the existence of the World-Soul, and a few words upon this subject are necessary. The soul, in Plato's system, is the mediator between the world of Ideas and the world of sense. Like the former, it is incorporeal and immortal. Like the latter, it occupies space. Plato thought that there must be a soul in the world to account for the rational behaviour of things, and to explain motion. The reason which governs and directs the world dwells in the World-Soul. And the World-Soul is the cause of motion in the outer universe, just as the human soul is the cause of the motions of the human body. The cosmos is a living being.

(b) The Doctrine of the Human Soul.

The human soul is similar in kind to the World-Soul. It is the cause of the body's movements, and in it the human reason dwells. It has affinities both with the world of Ideas and the world of sense. It is divided into two parts, of which one part is again subdivided into two. The highest part is reason, which is that part of the soul which apprehends the Ideas. It is simple and indivisible. Now all destruction of things means the sundering of their parts. But the rational part of the soul, being simple, has no parts. Therefore it is indestructible and immortal. The irrational part of the soul is mortal, and is subdivided into a noble and an ignoble half. To the noble half belong courage, love of honour, and in general the nobler emotions. To the ignoble portion belong the sensuous appetites. The noble half has a certain affinity with reason, in that it has an instinct for what is noble and great. Nevertheless, this is mere instinct, and is not rational. The seat of reason is the head, of the noble half of the lower soul, the breast, of the ignoble half, the lower part of the body. Man alone possesses the three parts of the soul. Animals possess the two lower parts, plants only the appetitive soul. What distinguishes man from the lower orders of creation is thus that he alone possesses reason.

Plato connects the doctrine of the immortality of the rational soul with the theory of Ideas by means of the doctrines of recollection and transmigration. According to the former doctrine, all knowledge is recollection of what was experienced by the soul in its disembodied state before birth. It must carefully be noted, however, that the word knowledge is here used in the special and restricted sense of Plato. Not everything that we should call knowledge is recollection. The sensuous element in my perception that this paper is white is not recollection, since, as being merely sensuous, it is not, in Plato's opinion, to be called knowledge. Here, as elsewhere, he confines the term to rational knowledge, that is to say, knowledge of the Ideas, though it is doubtful whether he is wholly consistent with himself in the matter, especially in regard to mathematical knowledge. It must also be noted that this doctrine has nothing in common with the Oriental doctrine of the memory of our past lives upon the earth. An example of this is found in the Buddhist Jàtakas, where the Buddha relates from memory many things that happened to him in the body in his previous births. Plato's doctrine is quite different. It refers only to recollection of the experiences of the soul in its disembodied state in the world of Ideas.

The reasons assigned by Plato for believing in this doctrine may be reduced to two. Firstly, knowledge of the Ideas cannot be derived from the senses, because the Idea is never pure in its sensuous manifestation, but always mixed. The one beauty, for example, is only found in experience mixed with the ugly. The second reason is more striking. And, if the doctrine of recollection is itself fantastic, this, the chief reason upon which Plato bases it, is interesting and important. He pointed out that mathematical knowledge seems to be innate in the mind. It is neither imparted to us by instruction, nor is it gained from experience. Plato, in fact, came within an ace of discovering what, in modern times, is called the distinction between necessary and contingent knowledge, a distinction which was made by Kant the basis of most far-reaching developments in philosophy. The character of necessity attaches to rational knowledge, but not to sensuous. To explain this distinction, we may take as our example of rational knowledge such a proposition as that two and two make four. This does not mean merely that, as a matter of fact, every two objects and every other two objects, with which we have tried the experiment, make four. It is not merely a fact, it is a necessity. It is not merely that two and two do make four, but that they must make four. It is inconceivable that they should not. We have not got to go and see whether, in each new case, they do so. We know beforehand that they will, because they must. It is quite otherwise with such a proposition as, "gold is yellow." There is no necessity about it. It is merely a fact. For all anybody can see to the contrary it might just as well be blue. There is nothing inconceivable about its being blue, as there is about two and two making five. Of course, that gold is yellow is no doubt a mechanical necessity, that is, it is determined by causes, and in that sense could not be otherwise. But it is not a logical necessity. It is not a logical contradiction to imagine blue gold, as it would be to imagine two and two making five. Any other proposition in mathematics possesses the same necessity. That the angles at the base of an isosceles triangle are equal is a necessary proposition. It could not be otherwise without contradiction. Its opposite is unthinkable. But that Socrates is standing is not a necessary truth. He might just as well be sitting.

Since a mathematical proposition is necessarily true, its truth is known without verification by experience. Having proved the proposition about the isosceles triangle, we do not go about measuring the angles of triangular objects to make sure there is no exception. We know it without any experience at all. And if we were sufficiently clever, we might even evolve mathematical knowledge out of the resources of our own minds, without its being told us by any teacher. That Caesar was stabbed by Brutus is a fact which no amount of cleverness could ever reveal to me. This information I can only get by being told it. But that the base angles of an isosceles triangle are equal I could discover by merely thinking about it. The proposition about Brutus is not a necessary proposition. It might be otherwise. And therefore I must be told whether it is true or not. But the proposition about the isosceles triangle is necessary, and therefore I can see that it must be true without being told.

Now Plato did not clearly make this distinction between necessary and non-necessary knowledge. But what he did perceive was that mathematical knowledge can be known without either experience or instruction. Kant afterwards gave a less fantastic explanation of these facts. But Plato concluded that such knowledge must be already present in the mind at birth. It must be recollected from a previous existence. It might be answered that, though this kind of knowledge is not gained from the experience of the senses, it may be gained from teaching. It may be imparted by another mind. We have to teach children mathematics, which we should not have to do if it were already in their minds. But Plato's answer is that when the teacher explains a geometrical theorem to the child, directly the child understands what is meant, he assents. He sees it for himself. But if the teacher explains that Lisbon is on the Tagus, the child cannot see that this is true for himself. He must either believe the word of the teacher, or he must go and see. In this case, therefore, the knowledge is really imparted from one mind to another. The teacher transfers to the child knowledge which the child does not possess. But the mathematical theorem is already present in the child's mind, and the process of teaching merely consists in making him see what he already potentially knows. He has only to look into his own mind to find it. This is what we mean by saying that the child sees it for himself.

In the "Meno" Plato attempts to give an experimental proof of the doctrine of recollection. Socrates is represented as talking to a slave-boy, who admittedly has no education in mathematics, and barely knows what a square is. By dint of skilful questioning Socrates elicits from the boy's mind a theorem about the properties of the square. The point of the argument is that Socrates tells him nothing at all. He imparts no information. He only asks questions. The boy's knowledge of the theorem, therefore, is not due to the teaching of Socrates, nor is it due to experience. It can only be recollection. But if knowledge is recollection, it may be asked, why is it that we do not remember at once? Why is the tedious process of education in mathematics necessary? Because the soul, descending from the world of Ideas into the body, has its knowledge dulled and almost blotted out by its immersion in the sensuous. It has forgotten, or it has only the dimmest and faintest recollection. It has to be reminded, and it takes a great effort to bring the half-lost ideas back to the mind. This process of being reminded is education.

With this, of course, is connected the doctrine of transmigration, which Plato took, no doubt, from the Pythagoreans. Most of the details of Plato's doctrine of transmigration are mere myth. Plato does not mean them seriously, as is shown by the fact that he gives quite different and inconsistent accounts of these details in different dialogues. What, in all probability, he did believe, however, may be summarized as follows. The soul is pre-existent as well as immortal. Its natural home is the world of Ideas, where at first it existed, without a body, in the pure and blissful contemplation of Ideas. But because it has affinities with the world of sense, it sinks down into a body. After death, if a man has lived a good life, and especially if he has cultivated the knowledge of Ideas, philosophy, the soul returns to its blissful abode in the world of Ideas, till, after a long period it again returns to earth in a body. Those who do evil suffer after death severe penalties, and are then reincarnated in the body of some being lower than themselves. A man may become a woman. Men may even, if their lives have been utterly sensual, pass into the bodies of animals.

5. Ethics

(a) The Ethics of the Individual

Just as Plato's theory of knowledge begins with a negative portion, designed to refute false theories of what truth is, so does his theory of morals begin with a negative portion, intended to refute false theories of what virtue is. These two negative departments of Plato's philosophy correspond in every way. As he was then engaged in showing that knowledge is not perception, as Protagoras thought, so he now urges that virtue is not the same as pleasure. And as knowledge is not mere right opinion, neither is virtue mere right action. The propositions that knowledge is perception, and that virtue is pleasure, are indeed only the same principle applied to different spheres of thought. For the Sophists whatever appeared true to the individual was true for that individual. This is the same as saying that knowledge is perception. For the Sophists, again, whatever appeared right to the individual was right for that individual. This is the same as saying that it is right for each man to do whatever he pleases. Virtue is defined as the pleasure of the individual. This consequence of the Sophistic principles was drawn both by many of the Sophists themselves, and later by the Cyrenaics.

As these two propositions are thus in fact only one principle, what Plato has said in refutation of the former provides also his refutation of the latter. The theory that virtue is pleasure has the same destructive influence upon morals as the theory that knowledge is perception had upon truth. We may thus shortly summarize Plato's arguments.

(1) As the Sophistic theory of truth destroys the objectivity of truth, so the doctrine that virtue is the pleasure of the individual destroys the objectivity of the good. Nothing is good in itself. Things are only good for me or for you. There results an absolute moral relativity, in which the idea of an objective standard of goodness totally disappears.

(2) This theory destroys the distinction between good and evil. Since the good is whatever the individual pleases, and since the pleasure of one individual is the displeasure of another, the same thing is both good and evil at the same time, good for one person and evil for another. Good and evil are therefore not distinct. They are the same.

(3) Pleasure is the satisfaction of our desires. Desires are merely feelings. This theory, therefore, founds morality upon feeling. But an objective morality cannot be founded upon what is peculiar to individuals. If the moral code is to be a law binding upon all men, it can only be founded upon that which is common to all men, the universal reason.

(4) The end of moral activity must fall within, and not outside, the moral act itself. Morality must have an intrinsic, not a merely extrinsic, value. We must not do right for the sake of something else. We must do right because it is right, and thus make virtue an end in itself. But the Sophistic theory places the end of morality outside morality. We are to do right, not for its own sake, but for the sake of pleasure. Morality is thus not an end in itself, but merely a means towards a further end.

Virtue, therefore, is not pleasure, any more than knowledge is perception. Likewise, just as knowledge is not right opinion, so virtue is not right action. Right opinion may be held upon wrong grounds, and right action may be performed on wrong grounds. For true virtue we must not only know what is right, but why it is right. True virtue is thus right action proceeding from a rational comprehension of true values. Hence there arises in Plato's philosophy a distinction between philosophic virtue and customary virtue. Philosophic virtue is founded upon reason, and understands the principle on which it acts. It is, in fact, action governed by principles. Customary virtue is right action proceeding from any other grounds, such as custom, habit, tradition, good impulses, benevolent feelings, instinctive goodness. Men do right merely because other people do it, because it is customary, and they do it without understanding the reasons for it. This is the virtue of the ordinary honest citizen, the "respectable" person. It is the virtue of bees and ants, who act as if rationally, but without any understanding of what they are doing. And Plato observes--no doubt with an intentional spice of humour--that such people may in the next life find themselves born as bees and ants. Plato denies philosophic virtue not only to the masses of men, but even to the best statesmen and politicians of Greece.

As true virtue is virtue which knows at what it is aiming, the knowledge of the nature of the highest aim becomes the chief question of ethics. What is the end of moral activity? Now we have just seen that that end must fall within, and not outside, the moral act. The end of goodness is the good. What, then, is the good? What is the supreme good, the summum bonum?

A note of warning is necessary before we enter upon the details of this problem. Plato frequently speaks of all moral activity aiming at, and ending in, happiness. With modern phrases ringing in our ears, we might easily suppose this to mean that Plato is a utilitarian. The utilitarianism of Bentham and Mill is distinguished by the fact that it places the end of morality in happiness. Yet Plato was not a utilitarian, and would unhesitatingly have condemned the theory of Mill. He would have found it identical in principle with the Sophistic doctrine that pleasure is the end of virtue. The only difference is that, whereas the Sophists identified virtue with the pleasure of the individual, Mill makes it the pleasure of the community. That act is right which leads to "the greatest happiness of the greatest number." In practice, of course, this makes a tremendous difference. But the principle is equally objectionable because, like the Sophistic theory, it founds morality upon mere feeling, instead of upon reason, and because it places the end of morality outside morality itself. Yet the formula of Mill, that the end of morals is happiness, seems the same as Plato's formula. What is the difference?

The fact is that what Mill calls happiness Plato would have called pleasure. Pleasure is the satisfaction of one's desires, whether they are noble or ignoble. Then what is happiness? It can only be defined as the general harmonious well-being of life. Only that man is happy whose soul is in the state it ought to be in, only in fact the just, the good, and the moral man. Happiness has nothing to do with pleasure. If you could conceive an absolutely just and upright man, who was yet weighed down with every possible misery and disaster, in whose life pleasure had no part, such a man would still be absolutely happy. Happiness is, therefore, in Plato, merely another name for the summum bonum. In saying that the summum bonum is happiness, Plato is not telling us anything about it. He is merely giving it a new name. And we are still left to enquire: what is the summum bonum? what is happiness?

Plato's answer, as indeed his whole ethics, is but an application of the theory of Ideas. But here we can distinguish two different and, to some extent, inconsistent strains of thought, which exist side by side in Plato, and perpetually struggle for the mastery. Both views depend upon the theory of Ideas. In the first place, the Idea, in Plato's philosophy, is the sole reality. The object of sense is unreal, and merely clogs and dims the soul's vision of the Ideas. Matter is that which obstructs the free activity of the Idea. Sense-objects hide the Idea from our view. Therefore the world of sense is wholly evil. True virtue must consist in flying from the world of sense, in retiring from the affairs of the world, and even from the beauty of the senses, into the calm of philosophic contemplation. And if this were all, philosophy, the knowledge of the Ideas, would be the sole constituent of the summum bonum. But it is possible to regard sense-objects in another light. They are, after all, copies of the Ideas. They are therefore a manifestation and revelation of the ideal world. Hence Plato is compelled by this thought to allow a certain value to the world of sense, its affairs, and its beauty.

The result of this inconsistency is, at any rate, that Plato remains broad and human. He does not, on the one hand, preach a purely selfish retirement into philosophy, or a narrow ascetic ideal. He does not, on the other hand, adopt a low utilitarian view of life, allowing value only to that which is "practical." He remains true to the Greek ideal of life as a harmonious play of all the faculties, in which no one part of man is over-developed at the expense of the others.

The result is that Plato's summum bonum is not a single end. It is a compound consisting of four parts. First, and chief of all, is the knowledge of the Ideas as they are in themselves, philosophy. Secondly, the contemplation of the Ideas as they reveal themselves in the world of sense, the love and appreciation of all that is beautiful, ordered, and harmonious. Thirdly, the cultivation of the special sciences and arts. And fourthly, indulgence in pure, refined, and innocent pleasures of the senses, excluding, of course, whatever is base and evil.

Plato had also a specific doctrine of virtue. As already stated, he distinguished between philosophic and customary virtue, and attached absolute value only to the former. He does not, however, deny a relative value to customary virtue, inasmuch as it is a means towards true virtue. Plato saw that man cannot rise at one bound to the pinnacles of rational virtue. He must needs pass through the preparatory stage of customary virtue. In the man in whom reason is not yet awakened, good habits and customs must be implanted, in order that, when reason comes, it may find the ground ready prepared.

Socrates had taught that virtue is one. And Plato in his earlier writings adopted this view. But later on he came to see that every faculty of man has its place and its function, and the due performance of its function is a virtue. He did not, however, surrender the unity of virtue altogether, but believed that its unity is compatible with its plurality. There are four cardinal virtues. Three of these correspond to the three parts of the soul, and the fourth is the unity of the others. The virtue of reason is wisdom, of the noble half of the mortal soul courage, of the ignoble appetites, temperance or self-control, in which the passions allow themselves to be governed by reason. The fourth virtue, justice, arises from the others. Justice means proportion and harmony, and accrues to the soul when all three parts perform their functions and co-operate with each other.

Following Zeller, we may add to this account of the virtues some of Plato's views upon the details of life. And first, his opinion of women and marriage. Here Plato does not rise above the level of ordinary Greek morals. He has nothing specially original to say, but reflects the opinions of his age. Women he regards as essentially inferior to men. Moreover, the modern view of woman as the complement of man, as possessing those special virtues of womanliness, which a man lacks, is quite alien to Plato. The difference between men and women is, in his view, not one of kind but only of degree. The only specific difference between the sexes is the physical difference. Spiritually they are quite the same, except that woman is inferior. Hence Plato would not exclude women from the same education which man receives. He would educate them in exactly the same way, but this involves the imposition upon them of the same burdens. Even military duties are not outside the sphere of women.

His views of marriage flow from the same principle. Since woman is not the complement of man, she is in no special sense fitted to be his companion. Hence the ideal of spiritual companionship is absent from Plato's view of marriage, the sole object of which, in his opinion, is the propagation of children. The natural companion of a man is not a woman, but another man. The ideal of friendship, therefore, takes the place of the spiritual ideal of marriage in Plato and, indeed, among the ancients generally.

Slavery is not denounced by Plato. He takes no trouble to justify it, because he thinks it so obviously right that it needs no justification. All that can be said to his credit is that he demands humane and just, though firm and unsentimental, treatment of slaves.

If in these respects Plato never transcends the Greek view of life, in one matter at least he does so. The common view of his time was that one ought to do good to one's friends and evil to one's enemies. This Plato expressly repudiates. It can never be good, he thinks, to do evil. One should rather do good to one's enemies, and so convert them into friends. To return good for evil is no less a Platonic than a Christian maxim.

(b) The State.

We pass from the ethics of individual life to the ethics of the community. Plato's "Republic" is not an attempt to paint an imaginary and unreal perfection. Its object is to found politics on the theory of Ideas by depicting the Idea of the State. This State is, therefore, not unreal, but the only real State, and its reality is the ground of the existence of all actually existent States.

We can trace here, too, the same two strains of thought as we found in considering the ethics of the individual. On the one hand, since the Idea alone is real, the existent world a mere illusion, the service of the State cannot be the ideal life for a rational being. Complete retirement from the world into the sphere of Ideas is a far nobler end, and the aims of the ordinary politician are, in comparison, worthless baubles. Though only the philosopher is competent to rule, yet he will not undertake the business of the State, except under compulsion. In the political States, as they exist in the world, the philosopher dwells with his body, but his soul is a stranger, ignorant of their standards, unmoved by their ambitions. But the opposite strain of thought is uppermost when we are told that it is, after all, only in the State, only in his capacity as a citizen and a social being that the individual can attain perfection. It is only possible to reconcile these views in one way. If the ideals of the State and of philosophy seem inconsistent, they must be brought together by adapting the State to philosophy. We must have a State founded upon philosophy and reason. Then only can the philosopher dwell in it with his soul as well as with his body. Then only can either the individual or the State reach perfection. To found the State upon reason is the keynote of Plato's politics.

And this gives us, too, the clue to the problem, what is the end of the State? Why should there be a State at all? This does not mean, how has the State arisen in history? We are not in search of the cause, but of the reason, or end, of the State. The end of all life is wisdom, virtue, and knowledge. The unassisted individual cannot reach these ends. It is only by the State that they can be brought down from heaven to earth. The end of the State is thus the virtue and happiness (not pleasure) of the citizens. And since this is only possible through education, the State's primary function is educational.

Since the State is to be founded upon reason, its laws must be rational, and rational laws can only be made by rational men, philosophers. The rulers must be philosophers. And since the philosophers are few, we must have an aristocracy, not of birth, or of wealth, but of intellect. The first operative principle of the State is reason, the second is force. For it is not to be expected that the irrational masses will willingly submit to rational laws. They must be compelled. And since the work of the world must go on, the third operative principle will be labour. Plato believed in the principle of division of labour. Only he can excel at any occupation whose life is devoted to it. Hence to the three operative principles correspond three classes, castes, or professions. Reason is embodied in the philosopher-rulers, force in the warriors, labour in the masses. This division of the functions of the State is based upon the threefold division of the soul. To the rational soul correspond the philosopher-rulers, to the nobler half of the mortal soul the warriors, to the appetitive soul the masses. Consequently the four cardinal virtues belong to the State through the functioning of the three classes. The virtue of the philosopher-rulers is wisdom, of the warriors courage, of the masses, temperance. The harmonious co-operation of all three produces justice.

The rulers must not cease to be philosophers. Most of their time must be spent in the study of the Ideas, philosophy, and only a portion in the affairs of government. This is rendered possible by the system of taking turns. Those who are not at any particular time engaged upon government retire into thought. The duty of the warriors is the protection of the State, both against its external enemies, and against the irrational impulses of the masses of its own citizens. Normally, the latter will be their chief duty, the enforcement of the decrees of the philosopher-rulers upon the masses. The masses will engage themselves in trade, commerce, and agriculture. Both the other ranks are prohibited from soiling their fingers with trade or agriculture, upon which Plato, as a Greek aristocrat, looked down with unbounded contempt. To what rank a citizen belongs is not determined by birth, nor by individual choice. No individual can choose his own profession. This will be determined by the officers of the State, who will base their decision, however, upon the disposition and capabilities of the individual. As they have also to decide the numbers required for each rank, the magistrates also control the birth of children. Parents cannot have children when they wish. The sanction of the State is required.

Since the end of the State is the virtue of the citizens, this involves the destruction of whatever is evil and the encouragement of whatever is good. To compass the destruction of evil, the children of bad parents, or offspring not sanctioned by the State, will be destroyed. Weak and sickly children will also not be allowed to live. The positive encouragement of good involves the education of the citizens by the State. Children from their earliest years do not belong to their parents, but to the State. They are, therefore, at once removed from the custody of their parents, and transferred to State nurseries. Since the parents are to have no property nor interest in them, stringent means are adopted to see that, after removal to the public nurseries, parents shall never again be able to recognize their own children. All the details of the educational curriculum are decreed by the State. Poetry, for example, is only allowed in an emasculated form. Of the three kinds, epic, dramatic, and lyric, the two former are banished from the State altogether, because, in the base example of the immorality of the gods, which they depict, they are powerful instruments in the propagation of evil. Only lyric poetry is allowed, and that under strict supervision. The subject, the form, even the metre, will be prescribed by the proper authorities. Poetry is not recognized as valuable in itself, but only as an educative moral influence. All poems, therefore, must strictly inculcate virtue.

It is, in Plato's opinion, intolerable that the individual should have any interest apart from the interests of the State. Private interests clash with those of the community, and must therefore be abolished. The individual can possess no property either in material things, or in the members of his family. This involves the community of goods, community of wives, and the State ownership of children from their birth.

6. Views upon Art.

In modern times aesthetics is recognized as a separate division of philosophy. This was not the case in Plato's time, and yet his opinions upon art cannot be fitted into either dialectic, physics, or ethics. On the other hand, they cannot be ignored, and there is nothing for it, therefore, but to treat them as a sort of appendix to his philosophy. Plato has no systematic theory of art, but only scattered opinions, the most important of which will now be mentioned.

Most modern theories of art are based upon the view that art is an end in itself, that the beautiful has, as such, absolute value, and not value merely as a means to some further end. Upon such a view, art is recognized as autonomous within its own sphere, governed only by its own laws, judged only by its own standards. It cannot be judged, as Tolstoi would have us believe, by the standard of morals. The beautiful is not a means to the good. They may be indeed, ultimately identical, but their identity cannot be recognized till their difference has been admitted. Nor can one be subordinated to the other.

Now this view of art finds no place at all in Plato's thought. Art is, for him, absolutely subservient both to morals and to philosophy. That it subserves morality we see from the "Republic," where only that poetry is allowed which inculcates virtue, and only because it inculcates virtue. It is no sufficient justification of a poem to plead that it is beautiful. Beautiful or not, if it does not subserve the ends of morality, it is forbidden. Hence too the preposterous notion that its exercise is to be controlled, even in details, by the State. That this would mean the utter destruction of art either did not occur to Plato, or if it did, did not deter him. If poetry cannot exist under the yoke of morality, it must not be allowed to exist at all. That art is merely a means to philosophy is even more evident. The end of all education is the knowledge of the Ideas, and every other subject, science, mathematics, art, is introduced into the educational curriculum solely as a preparation for that end. They have no value in themselves. This is obvious from the teaching of the "Republic," and it is even more evident in the "Symposium," where the love of beautiful objects is made to end, not in itself, but in philosophy.

Plato's low estimate of art appears also in his theory of art as imitation, and his contemptuous references to the nature of artistic genius. As to the first, art is, to him, only imitation. It is the copy of an object of the senses, and this again is only a copy of an Idea. Hence a work of art is only a copy of a copy. Plato did not recognise the creativeness of art. This view is certainly false. If the aims of art were merely to imitate, a photograph would be the best picture, since it is the most accurate copy of its object. What Plato failed to see was that the artist does not copy his object, but idealizes it. And this means that he does not see the object simply as an object, but as the revelation of an Idea. He does not see the phenomenon with the eyes of other men, but penetrates the sensuous envelope and exhibits the Idea shining through the veils of sense.

The second point is Plato's estimate of artistic genius. The artist does not work by reason, but by inspiration. He does not, or he should not, create the beautiful by means of rules, or by the application of principles. It is only after the work of art is created that the critic discovers rules in it. This does not mean that the discovery of rules is false, but that the artist follows them unconsciously and instinctively. If, for example, we believe Aristotle's dictum that the object of tragedy is to purge the heart by terror and pity, we do not mean that the tragedian deliberately sets out to accomplish that end. He does so without knowing or intending it. And this kind of instinctive impulse we call the inspiration of the artist. Now Plato fully recognizes these facts. But far from considering inspiration something exalted, he thinks it, on the contrary, comparatively low and contemptible, just because it is not rational. He calls it "divine madness," divine indeed, because the artist produces beautiful things, but madness because he himself does not know how or why he has done it. The poet says very wise and beautiful things, but he does not know why they are wise and beautiful. He merely feels, and does not understand anything. His inspiration, therefore, is not on the level of knowledge, but only of right opinion, which knows what is true, but does not know why.

Plato's views of art are thus not satisfactory. He is doubtless right in placing inspiration below reason, and art below philosophy. They do stand to each other in the relation of higher and lower. Not that such a question can be decided by mere personal preferences. The usual discussions whether art or philosophy is better, whether emotion or reason is higher, are pointless and insipid, because the disputants merely exalt their personal peculiarities. The man of artistic temperament naturally prefers art, and says it is the highest. The philosopher exalts philosophy above art, merely because it is his pet hobby. This kind of discussion is futile. The matter must be decided upon some principle. And the principle is quite clear. Both art and philosophy have the same object, the apprehension of the Absolute, or the Idea. Philosophy apprehends it as it is in itself, that is to say, as thought. Art apprehends it in a merely sensuous form. Philosophy apprehends it in its truth, art in a comparatively untrue way. Philosophy, therefore, is the higher. But while any true philosophy of art must recognize this, it must not interpret it to mean that art is to be made merely a means towards philosophy. It must somehow find room for the recognition of the truth that art is an end in itself, and it is in this that Plato fails.

Aristotle, who had no spark of artistic capacity in his composition, whose own writings are the severest of scientific treatises, did far greater justice to art than Plato, and propounded a far more satisfactory theory. Plato, himself a great artist, is utterly unjust to art. Paradoxical as it may appear, the very reason why Aristotle could be just to art was that he was no artist. Being solely a philosopher, his own writings are scientific and inartistic. This enables him to recognize art as a separate sphere, and therefore as having its own rights. Plato could not keep the two separate. His dialogues are both works of art and of philosophy. We have seen already that this fact exercised an evil influence on his philosophy, since it made him substitute poetic myths for scientific explanation. Now we see that it exercised an equally evil influence on his views of art. As a philosopher-artist his own practice is to use literary art solely as a means towards the expression of philosophical ideas. And this colours his whole view of art. It is, to him, nothing but a means towards philosophy. And this is the tap-root of his entire view of the subject.

7. Critical Estimate of Plato's Philosophy,

If we are to form a just estimate of the value of Plato's philosophy, we must not fritter away our criticism on the minor points, the external details, the mere outworks of the system. We must get at the heart and governing centre of it all. Amid the mass of thought which Plato has developed, in all departments of speculation, that which stands out as the central thesis of the whole system is the theory of Ideas. All else is but deduction from this. His physics, his ethics, his politics, his views upon art, all flow from this one governing theory. It is here then that we must look, alike for the merits and the defects of Plato's system.

The theory of Ideas is not a something sprung suddenly upon the world out of Plato's brain. It has its roots in the past. It is, as Aristotle showed, the outcome of Eleatic, Heracleitean, and Socratic determinations. Fundamentally, however, it grows out of the distinction between sense and reason, which had been the common property of Greek thinkers since the time of Parmenides. Parmenides was the first to emphasize this distinction, and to teach that the truth is to be found by reason, the world of sense being illusory. Heracleitus, and even Democritus, were pronounced adherents of reason, as against sense. The crisis came with the Sophists, who attempted to obliterate the distinction altogether, and to find all knowledge in sensation, thus calling forth the opposition of Socrates and Plato. As against them Socrates pointed out that all knowledge is through concepts, reason: and Plato added to this that the concept is not a mere rule of thought but a metaphysical reality. This was the substance of the theory of Ideas. Every philosophy which makes a systematic attempt to solve the riddle of the universe necessarily begins with a theory of the nature of that absolute and ultimate reality from which the universe is derived. This absolute reality we will call simply the Absolute. Plato's theory is that the

Absolute consists of concepts. To say that the Absolute is reason, is thought, is concepts, is the universal--these are merely four different expressions of the same theory. Now this proposition, that the Absolute is reason, is the fundamental thesis of all idealism. Since Plato's time there have been several great idealistic systems of philosophy. That the Absolute is reason is the central teaching of them all. Plato, therefore, is the founder and initiator of all idealism. It is this that gives him his great place in the history of philosophy. That the Absolute is universal thought, this is what Plato has contributed to the philosophical speculation of the world. This is his crowning merit.

But we must go somewhat more into details. We must see how far he applied this principle successfully to the unravelment of the great problems of philosophy. In lecturing upon the Eleatics, I said that any successful philosophy must satisfy at least two conditions. It must give such an account of the Absolute, that the Absolute is shown as capable of explaining the world. It must be possible to deduce the actual world of facts from the first principle. Secondly, not only must this first principle explain the world; it must also explain itself. It must be really ultimate, that is, we must not, in order to understand it, have to refer to anything beyond and outside it. If we have to do so then our ultimate is not an ultimate at all; our first principle is not first. That thing by means of which we explain it must itself be the ultimate reality. And besides being ultimate, our principle must be wholly intelligible. It must not be a mere ultimate mystery; for to reduce the whole world to an ultimate mystery is clearly not to explain it. Our first principle must, in a word, be self-explanatory. Let us apply this two-fold test to Plato's system. Let us see, firstly, whether the principle of Ideas explains the world, and secondly, whether it explains itself.

Does it explain the world? Is the actual existence of things, horses, trees, stars, men, explained by it? What, in the first place, is the relation between things and the Ideas? Things, says Plato, are "copies," or "imitations" of the Ideas. They "participate" in the Ideas. The Ideas are "archetypal" of things. Now all these phrases are mere poetic metaphors. They do not really tell us how things are related to Ideas. But suppose we ignore this, and assume, for the sake of argument, that we understand what is meant by "participation" and that things are, in the literal sense, "copies" of Ideas. The question still remains, why do such copies exist, how do they arise? Now, if this problem is to be solved, it is not enough to show, merely as a fact, that, by some mysterious act, copies of Ideas come into existence. There must be a reason for it, and this reason it is the business of philosophy to explain. This reason, too, must exist in the nature of the Ideas themselves, and not outside them. There must be, in the very nature of the Ideas, some inner necessity which forces them to reproduce themselves in things. This is what we mean by saying that the Ideas are a sufficient explanation of the existence of things. But there is in Plato's Ideas no such necessity. The Ideas are defined as being the sole reality. They have already all reality in themselves. They are self-sufficient. They lack nothing. It is not necessary for them further to realize their being in the concrete manifestation of things, because they, as wholly real, need no realization. Why, then, should they not remain for ever simply as they are? Why should they go out of themselves into things? Why should they not remain in themselves and by themselves? Why should they need to reproduce themselves in objects? There are, we know, white objects in the universe. Their existence, we are told, is explained by the Idea of whiteness? But why should the Idea of whiteness produce white things? It is itself the perfect whiteness. Why should it stir itself? Why should it not remain by itself, apart, sterile, in the world of Ideas, for all eternity? We cannot see. There is in the Ideas no necessity urging them towards reproduction of themselves, and this means that they possess no principle for the explanation of things.

Nevertheless Plato has to make some attempt to meet the difficulty. And as the Ideas are themselves impotent to produce things, Plato, unable to solve the problem by reason, attempts to solve it by violence. He drags in the notion of God from nowhere in particular, and uses him as a deus ex machina. God fashions matter into the images of Ideas. The very fact that Plato is forced to introduce a creator shows that, in the Ideas themselves, there is no ground of explanation. Things ought to be explained by the Ideas themselves, but as they are incapable of explaining anything, God is called upon to do their work for them. Thus Plato, faced with the problem of existence, practically deserts his theory of Ideas, and falls back upon a crude theism. Or if we say that the term God is not to be taken literally, and that Plato uses it merely as a figurative term for the Idea of Good, then this saves Plato from the charge of introducing a theism altogether inconsistent with his philosophy, but it brings us back to the old difficulty. For in this case, the existence of things must be explained by means of the Idea of the Good. But this Idea is just as impotent as the other Ideas.

In this connection, too, the dualism of Plato's system becomes evident. If everything is grounded in the one ultimate reality, the Ideas, then the entire universe must be clasped together in a system, all parts of which flow out of the Ideas. If there exists in the universe anything which stands aloof from this system, remains isolated, and cannot be reduced to a manifestation of the Ideas, then the philosophy has failed to explain the world, and we have before us a confessed dualism. Now not only has Plato to drag in God for the explanation of things, he has also to drag in matter. God takes matter and forms it into copies of the Ideas. But what is this matter, and where does it spring from? Clearly, if the sole reality is the Ideas, matter, like all else, must be grounded in the Ideas. But this is not the case in Plato's system. Matter appears as a principle quite independent of the Ideas. As its being is self-derived and original, it must be itself a substance. But this is just what Plato denies, calling it absolute not-being. Yet since it has not its source in the Ideas or in anything outside itself, we must say that though Plato calls it absolute not-being, it is in fact an absolute being. The Ideas and matter stand face to face in Plato's system neither derived from the other, equally ultimate co-ordinate, absolute realities. This is sheer dualism.

The source of this dualism is to be found in the absolute separation which Plato makes between sense and reason. He places the world of sense on one side, the world of reason on the other, as things radically different and opposed. Hence it is impossible for him ever to bridge the gulf that he has himself created between them. We may expect the dualism of a philosophy which builds upon such premises to break out at numerous points in the system. And so indeed it does. It exhibits itself as the dualism of Ideas and matter, of the sense-world and the thought-world, of body and soul. Not, of course, that it is not quite right to recognize the distinction between sense and reason. Any genuine philosophy must recognize that. And no doubt too it is right to place truth and reality on the side of reason rather than sense. But although sense and reason are distinct, they must also be identical. They must be divergent streams flowing from one source. And this means that a philosophy which considers the absolute reality to be reason must exhibit sense as a lower form of reason. Because Plato fails to see the identity of sense and reason, as well as their difference, his philosophy becomes a continual fruitless effort to overreach the dualism thus generated.

Thus the answer to our first question, whether the theory of Ideas explains the world of things, must be answered in the negative. Let us pass on to the second test. Is the principle of Ideas a self-explanatory principle? Such a principle must be understood purely out of itself. It must not be a principle, like that of the materialist, which merely reduces the whole universe to an ultimate mysterious fact. For even if it be shown that the reason of everything is matter, it is still open to us to ask what the reason of matter is. We cannot see any reason why matter should exist. It is a mere fact, which dogmatically forces itself upon our consciousness without giving any reason for itself. Our principle must be such that we cannot ask a further reason of it. It must be its own reason, and so in itself satisfy the demand for a final explanation. Now there is only one such principle in the world, namely, reason itself. You can ask the reason of everything else in the world. You can ask the reason of the sun, the moon, stars, the soul, God, or the devil. But you cannot ask the reason of reason, because reason is its own reason. Let us put the same thought in another way. When we demand the explanation of anything, what do we mean by explanation? What is it we want? Do we not mean that the thing appears to us irrational, and we want it shown that it is rational? When this is done, we say it is explained. Think, for example, of what is called the problem of evil. People often talk of it as the problem of the "origin of evil," as if what we want to know is, how evil began. But even if we knew this, it would not explain anything. Suppose that evil began because someone ate an apple. Does this make the matter any clearer? Do we feel that all our difficulties about the existence of evil are solved? No. This is not what we want to know. The difficulty is that evil appears to us something irrational. The problem can only be solved by showing us that somehow, in spite of appearances, it is rational that evil should exist. Show us this, and evil is explained. Explanation of a thing, then, means showing that the thing is rational. Now we can ask that everything else in the world should be shown to be rational. But we cannot demand that the philosopher shall show that reason is rational. This is absurd. Reason is what is already absolutely rational. It is what explains itself. It is its own reason. It is a self-explanatory principle. This, then, must be the principle of which we are in search. The Absolute, we said, must be a self-explanatory principle, and there is only one such, namely, reason. The Absolute, therefore, is reason.

It was the greatness and glory of Plato to have seen this, and thereby to have become the founder of all true philosophy. For to say that the Absolute is concepts is the same as saying it is reason. It might seem, then, that Plato has satisfied the second canon of criticism. He takes as first principle a self-explanatory reality. But we cannot quite so quickly jump to this conclusion. After all, the mere word reason is not a key which will unlock to us the doors of the universe. Something more is necessary than the mere word. We must, in fact, be told what reason is. Now there are two senses in which we might ask the question, what reason is, one of which is legitimate, the other illegitimate. It is illegitimate to ask what reason is, in the sense of asking that it shall be explained to us in terms of something else, which is not reason. This would be to give up our belief that reason is its own reason. It would be to seek the reason of reason in something which is not reason. It would be to admit that reason, in itself, is not rational. And this is absurd. But it is legitimate to ask, what reason is, meaning thereby, what is the content of reason. The content of reason, we have seen, is concepts. But what concepts? How are we to know whether any particular concept is part of the system of reason or not? Only, it is evident, by ascertaining whether it is a rational concept. If a concept is wholly rational, then it is a part of reason. If not, not. What we need, then, is a detailed account of all the concepts which reason contains, and a proof that each of these concepts is really rational. It is obvious that only in this way can we make a satisfactory beginning in philosophy. Before we can show that reason explains, that is, rationalizes the world, we must surely first show that reason itself is rational, or rather, to be more accurate, that our conception of reason is rational. There must not be any mere inexplicable facts, any mysteries, any dark places, in our notion of reason. It must be penetrated through and through by the light of reason. It must be absolutely transparent, crystalline. How can we hope to explain the world, if our very first principle itself contains irrationalities?

Each concept then must prove itself rational. And this means that it must be a necessary concept. A necessary proposition, we saw, is one, such as that two and two equal four, the opposite of which is unthinkable. So for Plato's Ideas to be really necessary it ought to be logically impossible for us to deny their reality. It ought to be impossible to think the world at all without these concepts. To attempt to deny them ought to be shown to be self-contradictory. They ought to be so necessarily involved in reason that thought without them becomes impossible. Clearly this is the same as saying that the Ideas must not be mere ultimate inexplicable facts. Of such a fact we assert merely that it is so, but we cannot see any reason for it. To see a reason for it is the same as seeing its necessity, seeing not merely that it is so, but that it must be so.

Now Plato's Ideas are not of this necessary kind. There is, we are told, an Idea of whiteness. But why should there be such an Idea? It is a mere fact. It is not a necessity. We can think the world quite well without the Idea of whiteness. The world, so far as we can see, could get on perfectly well without either white objects or the Idea of whiteness. To deny its reality leads to no self-contradictions. Put it in another way. There are certainly white objects in the world. We demand that these, among other things, be explained. Plato tells us, by way of explanation, that there are white objects because there is an Idea of whiteness. But in that case why is there an Idea of whiteness? We cannot see. There is no reason. There is no necessity in this. The same thing applies to all the other Ideas. They are not rational concepts. They are not a part of the system of reason.

But at this point, perhaps, a glimmer of hope dawns upon us. We ask the reason for these Ideas. Has not Plato asserted that the ultimate reason and ground of all the lower Ideas will be found in the supreme Idea of the Good? Now if this is so, it means that the lower Ideas must find their necessity in the highest Idea. If we could see that the Idea of the Good necessarily involves the other Ideas, then these other Ideas would be really explained. In other words, we ought to be able to deduce all the other Ideas from this one Idea. It ought to be possible to show that, granted the Idea of the Good, all the other Ideas necessarily follow, that to assume the Good and deny the other Ideas would be self-contradictory and unthinkable. There are examples in Plato of the kind of deduction we require. For example, in the "Parmenides" he showed that the Idea of the one necessarily involves the Idea of the many, and vice versa. You cannot think the one without also thinking the many. This means that the many is deduced from the one, and the one from the many. Just in the same way, we ought to be able to deduce the Idea of whiteness from the Idea of the Good. But this is clearly not possible. You may analyse the Good as long as you like, you may turn it in every conceivable direction, but you cannot get whiteness out of it. The two Ideas do not involve each other. They are thinkable apart. It is quite possible to think the Good without thinking whiteness. And it is the same with all the other Ideas. None of them can be deduced from the Good.

And the reason of this is very obvious. Just as the lower Ideas contain only what is common among the things of a class, and exclude their differences, so the higher Ideas include what is common to the Ideas that come under them, but exclude what is not common. For example, the Idea of colour contains what white, blue, red, and green, have in common. But all colours have not whiteness in common. Green, for example, is not white. Hence the Idea of colour excludes the Idea of whiteness, and it likewise excludes all the Ideas of the other particular colours. So too the highest Idea of all contains only what all the Ideas agree in, but all the rest falls outside it.

Thus the Idea of whiteness is perfect in its kind. And as all Ideas are likewise perfect, the highest Idea is that in which they all agree, namely, perfection itself. But this means that the perfection of the Idea of whiteness is contained in the supreme Idea, but its specific character in which it differs from other Ideas is excluded. Its specific character is just its whiteness. Thus the perfection of whiteness is contained in the Good, but its whiteness is not. Consequently it is impossible to deduce whiteness from the Good, because the Good does not contain whiteness. You cannot get out of it what is not in it. When Plato deduced the many from the one, he did so only by showing that the One contains the many. He cannot deduce whiteness from goodness, because goodness does not contain whiteness.

The lower Ideas thus have not the character of necessity. They are mere facts. And the hope that we shall find their necessity in the supreme Idea fails. But suppose we waive this. Suppose we grant that there must be an Idea of whiteness, because there is an Idea of the Good. Then why is there an Idea of the Good? What is the necessity of that? We cannot see any necessity in it. What we said of the other Ideas applies with equal force to the highest Idea. The Good may be a necessary Idea, but Plato has not shown it.

Thus, though Plato named reason as the Absolute, and though reason is a self-explanatory principle, his account of the detailed content of reason is so unsatisfactory that none of the concepts which he includes in it are really shown to be rational. His philosophy breaks down upon the second test as it did upon the first. He has neither explained the world from the Ideas, nor has he made the Ideas explain themselves.

There is one other defect in Plato's system which is of capital importance. There runs throughout it a confusion between the notions of reality and existence. To distinguish between existence and reality is an essential feature of all idealism. Even if we go back to the dim idealism of the Eleatics, we shall see this. Zeno, we saw, denied motion, multiplicity, and the world of sense. But he did not deny the existence of the world. That is an impossibility. Even if the world is delusion, the delusion exists. What he denied was the reality of existence. But if reality is not existence, what is it? It is Being, replied the Eleatics. But Being does not exist. Whatever exists is this or that particular sort of being. Being itself is not anywhere to be found. Thus the Eleatics first denied that existence is reality, and then that reality exists. They did not themselves draw this conclusion, but it is involved in their whole position.

With a fully developed idealism, like Plato's, this ought to be still clearer. And, in a sense, it is. The individual horse is not real. But it certainly exists. The universal horse is real. But it does not exist. But, upon this last point, Plato wavered and fell. He cannot resist the temptation to think of the absolute reality as existing. And consequently the Ideas are not merely thought as the real universal in the world, but as having a separate existence in a world of their own. Plato must have realised what is, in truth, involved in his whole position, that the absolute reality has no existence. For he tells us that it is the universal, and not any particular individual thing. But everything that exists is an individual thing. Again, he tells us that the Idea is outside time. But whatever exists must exist at some time. Here then this central idealistic thought seems well fixed in Plato's mind. But when he goes on to speak of recollection and reincarnation, when he tells us that the soul before birth dwelt apart in the world of Ideas, to which after death it may hope to return, it is clear that Plato has forgotten his own philosophy, that he is now thinking of the Ideas as individual existences in a world of their own. This is a world of Ideas having a separate existence and place of its own. It is not this world. It is a world beyond. Thus the Platonic philosophy which began on a high level of idealistic thinking, proclaiming the sole reality of the universal, ends by turning the universal itself into nothing but an existent particular. It is the old old story of trying to form mental pictures of that which no picture is adequate to comprehend. Since all pictures are formed out of sensuous materials, and since we can form no picture of anything that is not an individual thing, to form a picture of the universal necessarily means thinking of it as just what it is not, an individual. So Plato commits the greatest sin that can be ascribed to a philosopher. He treats thought as a thing.

To sum up. Plato is the great founder of idealism, the initiator of all subsequent truths in philosophy. But, as always with pioneers, his idealism is crude. It cannot explain the world; it cannot explain itself. It cannot even keep true to its own principles, because, having for the first time in history definitely enunciated the truth that reality is the universal, it straightway forgets its own creed and plunges back into a particularism which regards the Ideas as existent individuals. It was these defects which Aristotle set himself to rectify in a purer idealism, shorn of Plato's impurities.

www.ingramcontent.com/pod-product-compliance
Lightning Source LLC
Chambersburg PA
CBHW081617100526
44590CB00021B/3479